The Native Tongues Review

marcus "iomos marad" singleton

MC Till

Beau Brown

Donald "Profound" DeVold

Joe "Joe November" Thomas

Dayne Hall (Haz)

Jason Cuthbert

Michael Stover

Cover Artwork by Phat Hentoff

Edited by Header, Joe Thomas, and Beau Brown

Copyright © 2022 Everybody's Hip-Hop
All rights reserved.
ISBN: 9798837337505

Dedicated to Phife and Chris Lighty

CONTENTS

		Introductory Stuff	7
Pt. 1		**The Native Tongues Lists**	9
	1	The Top 100 Songs According to the Native Tongues Fan Group	11
	2	iomos marad	15
	3	MC Till	18
	4	Joe November	20
	5	Profound	23
	6	Beau Brown	25
Pt. 2		**Retrospectives & Reviews**	29
	7	1988: *Straight Out The Jungle* - Jungle Brothers	30
	8	1989: *3 Feet High and Rising* - De La Soul	From The Soul Comes DA Inner Sound Y'all (DAISY)	35
	9	1989: *All Hail the Queen* - Queen Latifah	45
	10	1990: *People's Instinctive Travels...* - A Tribe Called Quest	47
	11	1990: *Down to Earth* - Monie Love	49
	12	1991: *De La Soul is Dead* - De La Soul	52
	13	1991: *The Low End Theory* - A Tribe Called Quest	55
	14	1991: *A Wolf in Sheep's Clothing* - Black Sheep	A Wolf in Sheep's Clothing Wrapped in a Conundrum	58
	15	1993: *Midnight Marauders* Pt. 1 - A Tribe Called Quest	63
	16	1993: *Midnight Marauders* Pt. 2 - A Tribe Called Quest	71
	17	1993: *Buhloone Mindstate* - De La Soul	76
	18	1996: *Stakes is High* - De La Soul	80
	19	1996: *Beats, Rhymes & Life* - A Tribe Called Quest	83
	20	Sept 29, 1998: *The Love Movement*, the *Foundation*, & the *Black Star* - A Tribe Called Quest, Brand Nubian, Black Star	A Great Day for Natives	86

21	2004: *The Grind Date* - De La Soul	90
22	2016: *We Got it from Here..., And The Anonymous Nobody...* - A Tribe Called Quest, De La Soul | A Tale of Two Returns	94
23	2021: *Here Goes Nothing* - Shortie No Mass	98
24	2022: *Forever* - Phife Dawg	101

Pt. 3	**Essays**	**105**
25	The Native Tongues Name	106
26	3 Feet to 3 Decades: A Journey into Hip-Hop	112
27	An Ode to Phife	115
28	The Incredible Pieces of Phife	118
29	Why Posdnous is the Best	130
30	Bob Power	142
31	A Letter to DJ Red Alert	147
32	The First Ladies of the Native Tongues	153

Pt. 4	**Live Interviews**	**165**
33	Mike G of the Jungle Brothers	166
34	Dres of Black Sheep	182
35	Shortie No Mass	197

Pt. 5	**Written Interviews**	**215**
36	Chip-Fu	216
37	Masta Ace	221
38	Phat Hentoff	224
39	Wordsworth	228
40	Dug Infinite	233

INTRODUCTORY STUFF

Welcome to *The Native Tongues Review*. This book exists because we all love the Native Tongues. For most of us at Everybody's Hip-Hop Label, our favorite album is from a Native Tongues group and some of our favorite emcees are from the collective as well. The music of the Native Tongues helped inform our worldview and definitely our artistic lens more than any other artist or group on Earth. Thus, this book is primarily about the Native Tongues music and albums we love so much.

For the purpose of this book, we primarily explored albums, songs, and whatnots from the Jungle Brothers, De La Soul, A Tribe Called Quest, Queen Latifah, Monie Love, Black Sheep, and Chi-Ali. We are not pretending to be the authority on all things Native Tongues. Rather, we just love their music and want to explore and celebrate it. We are aware that several more groups and artists are often included as Native Tongues members. In preparing for this book, we asked a lot of people about who is and who isn't a member. We heard from fans and artists that have inside knowledge. We also heard from a few folks who were there during the Native Tongues heyday as well as official members of the group. Recurring names outside of who we cover in this book include The Beatnuts, Brand Nubian, Leaders of the New School, Da Bush Babees, Common, and Mos Def. That is a pretty spectacular list right there. We might just have to write another volume of this Native Tongues Review!

While this book is a celebration of the Native Tongues' music, it is not an attempt to document their overall impact on Hip-Hop culture. We write an annual book that looks at the best albums from that particular year. We reflect on a number of those albums and write about them. We also include retrospective pieces and Hip-Hop essays. However, the main objective of those annual books is to celebrate the dope music and artists from that year. That is what we are doing with this book, but instead of capturing one year's worth of music we are looking at one collective's worth of music. We did not reflect on every single Native Tongues release nor did we have a scientific method of which albums to cover. This is music, not rules and regulations. We love this music, so we naturally let the music guide us.

May this book be one more document that bears witness to the greatest Hip-Hop collective this world has ever heard. *We* think it is the greatest, at least. Thank you to the Native Tongues Collective for providing us with decades of inspiration. Rest in Peace to Phife always.

Peace,

MC Till and the Boom Bap Review Crew

Part One
The Native Tongues Lists

CHAPTER ONE
The Top 100 Native Tongues Songs

We moderate a Facebook group called *The Native Tongues Fan Group*. We invited this group to help us with a month-long crowd-sourced project to create a top 100 Native Tongues Songs List. This list is not what just a few people think. It is what a source of about 75 fellow Native Tongues enthusiasts think collectively. First, we asked members of the group to post their top 10ish favorite Native Tongues songs. We then sifted through all those lists and found the top 32. We offered a 32-song bracket style competition where members voted on a song vs song poll every day for a month. During that time, we also listed the other 68 songs based on those original top 10 lists and asked the group to vote on all 68. These two methods gave us the top 100 crowd-sourced Native Tongues songs of all time.

1. "Stakes is High" by De La Soul
2. "Award Tour" by A Tribe Called Quest
3. "The Choice is Yours" by Black Sheep
4. "Check the Rhime" by A Tribe Called Quest
5. "Buddy" by A Tribe Called Quest
6. "Scenario" by A Tribe Called Quest
7. "Me, Myself, & I" by De La Soul
8. "Breakadawn" by De La Soul
9. "Buddy (Remix)" by De La Soul
10. "U.N.I.T.Y." by Queen Latifah
11. "Ego Trippin (Part 2)" by De La Soul

12. "Find a Way" by A Tribe Called Quest
13. "Saturdays" by De La Soul
14. "Flavor of the Month" by Black Sheep
15. "Itzsoweezee" by De La Soul
16. "Ladies First" by Queen Latifah
17. "Strobelight Honey" by Black Sheep
18. "Monie in the Middle" by Monie Love
19. "Jazz" by A Tribe Called Quest
20. "Similak Child" by Black Sheep
21. "Roadrunner" by Chi-Ali
22. "Electric Relaxation" by A Tribe Called Quest
23. "Doin' Our Own Dang" by Jungle Brothers
24. "Excursions" by A Tribe Called Quest
25. "Just Another Day" by Queen Latifah
26. "Lyrics to Go" by A Tribe Called Quest
27. "Brain" by Jungle Brothers
28. "It's a Shame" by Monie Love
29. "Footprints" by A Tribe Called Quest
30. "I'll House You" by Jungle Brothers
31. "Black Hand Side" by Queen Latifah
32. "Wrath of my Madness" by Queen Latifah
33. "Bonita Applebum" by A Tribe Called Quest
34. "Can I Kick It?" by A Tribe Called Quest
35. "Potholes in my Lawn" by De La Soul
36. "Millie Pulled a Pistol on Santa" by De La Soul
37. "Buggin' Out" by A Tribe Called Quest
38. "Rock Co. Kane Flow" by De La Soul
39. "Butta" by A Tribe Called Quest
40. "Supa Emcees" by De La Soul
41. "Plug Tunin'" by De La Soul
42. "Oh My God" by A Tribe Called Quest
43. "Oodles of O's" by De La soul
44. "Ring, Ring, Ring" by De La Soul
45. "Say No Go" by De La Soul
46. "Scenario (Remix)" by A Tribe Called Quest

47. "Bitties in the BK Lounge" by De La Soul
48. "Stressed Out" by A Tribe Called Quest
49. "Sucka N****" by A Tribe Called Quest
50. "Verses from the Abstract" by A Tribe Called Quest
51. "I Left My Wallet in El Segundo" by A Tribe Called Quest
52. "We Can Get Down" by A Tribe Called Quest
53. "Oooh" by De La Soul
54. "Without a Doubt" by Black Sheep
55. "Age Ain't Nuthin' but a #" by Chi-Ali
56. "J Beez Comin Through" by Jungle Brothers
57. "Jimbrowski" by Jungle Brothers
58. "Big Brother Beat" by De La Soul
59. "Midnight" by A Tribe Called Quest
60. "I Am I Be" by De La Soul
61. "Black is Black" by Jungle Brothers
62. "Autobiographical" by Black Sheep
63. "Let the Horns Blow" by Chi-Ali
64. "To Whom it May Concern" by Black Sheep
65. "The Promo (Remix)" by Jungle Brothers
66. "Strobelight Honey (No We Didn't Mix)" by Black Sheep
67. "Similak Child (Remix)" by Black Sheep
68. "If the Papes Come" by A Tribe Called Quest
69. "Princess of the Posse (Remix)" by Queen Latifah
70. "I'm Gonna Do You" by Jungle Brothers
71. "Description of a Fool" by A Tribe Called Quest
72. "Beyond this World" by Jungle Brothers
73. "Keeping the Faith" by De La Soul
74. "My Writes" by De La Soul
75. "Phony Rappers" by A Tribe Called Quest
76. "D.A.I.S.Y. Age" by De La Soul
77. "Afro Connections at the Hi 5" by De La Soul
78. "Get a Hold" by A Tribe Called Quest
79. "Detrimentally Stable" by Monie Love
80. "I Can Do This" by Monie Love
81. "Pubic Enemy" by A Tribe Called Quest

82. "What U Waitin 4" by Jungle Brothers
83. "Fanatic of the B Word" by De La Soul
84. "Grandpa's Party" by Monie Love
85. "The Future" by De La Soul
86. "In Dayz 2 Come" by Jungle Brothers
87. "Acknowledge Your Own History" by Jungle Brothers
88. "In My Room" by Chi-Ali
89. "Lovely How I Let my Mind Flow" by De La Soul
90. "Sunshine" by De La Soul
91. "God It" by De La Soul
92. "U Make Me Sweat" by Jungle Brothers
93. "Shoomp" by De La Soul
94. "My Jimmy Weighs a Ton" by Jungle Brothers
95. "Back on the Wall" by Black Sheep
96. "Full Term Love" by Monie Love
97. "How Ya Want It We Got It" by Jungle Brothers
98. "Return of DST" by De La Soul
99. "Candy" by Jungle Brothers
100. "If It Wasn't for You" by De La Soul

CHAPTER TWO
iomos marad's LISTS

**iomos marad's
Top 10 Albums Connected to the Native Tongues**

- *All For One*—Brand Nubian (1990)
- *A Future Without A Past* —Leaders of the New School (1991)
- *Resurrection* —Common (1994)
- *Labcabincalifornia* —The Pharcyde (1995)
- *The Infamous* —Mobb Deep (1995)
- *Gravity* —Bush Babees (1996)
- *Black Star*—Mos Def & Talib Kweli (1998)
- *Black on Both Sides* —Mos Def (1999)
- *Fantastic Vol. 2* —Slum Village (2000)
- *Train of Thought* —Reflection Eternal (2000)

I know. I know. I know. I know what you all are thinking as you look at my top ten list. "This dude does not know what he is talking about with his top ten list!" I apologize in advance for anyone that I have offended by this blasphemous list but hear me out. I based my top ten list on two important reasons: (1) Albums that I go back to frequently when I'm about to write or work on a project for inspiration and (2) because I am a drummer, I am a beats type of guy and not just any beats. The beats must have a certain feel, swing and energy to them. For anyone who knows me, they know that I am a huge admirer of J Dilla and I think he is most definitely a Jeen-Yuhs—so it should not be a surprise that Slum Village is on my list. The beats on that album are timeless in my humble opinion. The Bush Babees *Gravity* album is on my list because I think that is one of the most slept on boom bap albums of all time (again, this is my humble opinion). I included the Pharcyde album because of "Drop" and "Runnin Away" (Dilla). All I can say about the *Black Star*, *Train of Thought*, and *Black on Both Sides* albums is that they are from the Rawkus era, and that era really shaped who I am as a human being, emcee, and artist overall. Thanks for checking out my top 10. peace.

iomos marad's Top 10 Native Tongues Singles

- "She.Fe.Mc's" - De La Soul (*Clear Lake Auditorium* EP)
- "The Bizness" - De La Soul feat. Common (*Stakes is High*)
- "Mr. Incognito" - A Tribe Called Quest (*Hits, Rarities & Remixes*)
- "Lovely How I Let My Mind Float" - De La Soul feat. Biz Markie (*Breakadawn* Single B-Side)
- "One Two Sh*t" - A Tribe Called Quest feat. Busta Rhymes (*Hits, Rarities & Remixes*)
- "On the Road Again Remix" - Jungle Brothers (*On the Road Again / Simple as That* 12" Single)
- "Oh My God Remix" - A Tribe Called Quest (*Hits, Rarities & Remixes*)
- "Stakes Is High Remix" - De La Soul feat. Truth Enola & Mos Def (*Itzsoweezee* 12" Single B-Side)
- "The Love Song" - Bush Babees feat. De La Soul & Mos Def (*Gravity*)
- "How You Want It We Got It Native Tongues Remix" - Jungle Brothers feat. De La Soul & Q-Tip (*Raw Deluxe*)

Honorable Mention:

- "Scenario Remix" - A Tribe Called Quest feat. Leaders of the New School & Kid Hood
- "Undisputed Champs" - Del the Funky Homosapien feat. Pep Love & Q-Tip
- "Crosstown Beef Bw Fa La Lashe" - Medina Green

This top ten list is dedicated to the B-Side songs era. I have always been a fan of B-Side jawns (even if the A-Side jawn sounded like a B-Side jawn) ever since I can remember. Please light some incense, get whatever you indulge in drink-wise, dim the lights, and vibe out to this top ten. peace.

iomos marad's Top Ten Native Tongues Videos

- "Jazz (We've Got)" / "Buggin' Out" - A Tribe Called Quest
- "Oh My God" - A Tribe Called Quest
- "Electric Relaxation" - A Tribe Called Quest
- "Check the Rhime" - A Tribe Called Quest
- "The Choice Is Yours" - Black Sheep
- "Itzsoweezee" - De La Soul
- "Oooh" - De La Soul feat. Rah Digga & Redman
- "Stakes Is High" - De La Soul
- "Shopping Bags" - De La Soul
- "Phat Phat" - De La Soul

CHAPTER THREE
MC TILL'S LISTS

MC Till's Top Ten Favorite Native Tongues albums

1. *Buhloone Mindstate* - De La Soul (1993)
2. *The Low End Theory* - A Tribe Called Quest (1991)
3. *Midnight Marauders* - A Tribe Called Quest (1993)
4. *A Wolf in Sheep's Clothing* - Black Sheep (1991)
5. *Stakes is High* - De La Soul (1996)
6. *Done by the Forces of Nature* - Jungle Brothers (1989)
7. *De La Soul is Dead* - De La Soul (1991)
8. *Non-Fiction* - Black Sheep (1994)
9. *Beats, Rhymes & Life* - A Tribe Called Quest (1996)
10. *3 Feet High & Rising* - De La Soul (1989)

I thought about trying to do an unbiased, analytical approach to what I intellectually think are the top ten best Native Tongues albums. I'm sorry, I'm just too attached to this collective to do that. So I sat down and thought about which Native Tongues albums I go back to the most. This is that list. It might change a bit here and there but for the most part, these ten albums stay in permanent rotation for me, as do all De La, Tribe, Jungle Brothers, and Black Sheep albums plus Dres solo albums, Monie Love's first album and The Legion CD and Chi-Ali and etc... I'm kind of a fan:)

MC Till's Top Ten Favorite Native Tongues Songs from His Top Ten Favorite Native Tongues Albums (in order of albums listed)

1. "I Am, I Be" - De La Soul (*Buhloone Mindstate*)
2. "Show Business" - A Tribe Called Quest featuring Sadat X, Lord Jamar, & Diamond D (*The Low End Theory*)
3. "Steve Biko" - A Tribe Called Quest (*Midnight Marauders*)
4. "The Choice is Yours" - Black Sheep (*A Wolf in Sheep's Clothing*)
5. "Stakes is High" - De La Soul (*Stakes is High*)
6. "Doin our Own Dang" - Jungle Brothers featuring De La Soul, Q-Tip, & Monie Love (*Done by the Forces of Nature*)
7. "Bitties in the BK Lounge" - De La Soul (*De La Soul is Dead*)
8. "Without a Doubt" - Black Sheep (*Non-Fiction*)
9. "The Pressure" - A Tribe Called Quest (*Beats, Rhymes & Life*)
10. "Change in Speak" - De La Soul (*3 Feet High & Rising*)

I had so many different lists going. Top ten favorite songs that feature Dres. Top ten De La Soul songs. Top ten songs that feature Native Tongues emcees but are not from Native Tongues albums and many more list ideas. But at the end of the day, I decided to keep it simple. I looked at my top ten favorite Native Tongues albums and found a song from each of those albums that always stands out to me.

CHAPTER FOUR
JOE NOVEMBER'S LISTS

Joe November's Top Ten Native Tongues Albums

- *The Low End Theory* - A Tribe Called Quest (1991)
- *De La Soul Is Dead* - De La Soul (1991)
- *Midnight Marauders* - A Tribe Called Quest (1993)
- *A Wolf in Sheep's Clothing* - Black Sheep (1991)
- *The Fabulous Chi-Ali* - Chi-Ali (1992)
- *Black Reign* - Queen Latifah (1993)
- *Straight Out The Jungle* - Jungle Brothers (1989)
- *The Grind Date* - De La Soul (2004)
- *Forever* - Phife Dawg (2022)
- *The Beatnuts: Street Level* - The Beatnuts (1994)

This was probably one of the hardest lists I've ever had to put together. There are so many great Native Tongues albums, how can I possibly narrow them down? Well, the first five albums I listed were played in my tape deck/CD player/mp3 player so many times during my youth that there's no way I could ignore them. Top 5 Dead or Alive, as the kids might say. So let's look at albums six through ten. Queen Latifah's album had a huge impact on me because prior to its release, my perception of her was limited to a very superficial "pro-feminist ladies first 'I'm so sick of y'all that I've had it up to here'" persona that didn't do her much justice at all. *Black Reign* changed all that for me because it showed she was so much more than that. She was Hip-Hop through and through, and wow could she sing! She could rhyme over so many different styles, and she has such a commanding voice. I wasn't a huge Jungle Brothers fan early on. I had only heard "Because I Got It Like That" on some rap compilation and thought "meh...". Incidentally, that same compilation included De La's "Plug Tunin' (Last Chance to Comprehend)" which had me like "yoooo who is that?!" That triggered my love for De La right then and there. Anyway, I was much older when I went back and dug further into the Jungle Brothers catalog and realized how influential to Hip-Hop the JBs really were. *Straight Out The Jungle* to me is the grandfather of the Native Tongues family because it spawned the sampling style and lyricism I grew to love from subsequent Native Tongues albums. It had an earthy afro-centric vibe that I regret missing out on when the album first came out. I gain much more appreciation for it as I get older as well, sort of like how music can trigger a nostalgia for a time long since passed. Hip-Hop seemed simpler then, more fun. *The Grind Date* came out when I was a working adult in the armed forces overseas, and copping that CD made me feel that much closer to home. My Top 3 favorites from that LP are "Church'" "He Comes'" and of course, "Much More". Phife Dawg's posthumous release is not merely a sentimental entry; it reflects "grown man rap" for a lot of us Gen Xers who have kids, are married, and still love Hip-Hop over any other music genre. I grew up with Phife, and he grew up with me. Plus, his candidness about his life's mistakes and struggles with diabetes showed me how far he had grown as an emcee, a husband, and a father. Due to all of this, Phife's album quickly shot up my Top Ten list. To round out the list, I wanted to pick an album from a group that is not considered "core" Native Tongues but more "peripheral," to reflect the level of influence the crew had on other artists around them. When *The Beatnuts: Street Level* released, I had just graduated high school and was about to embark on my journey into the US Air Force. I played this CD out in my Chevy

S-10 Silverado that summer. This album had dope beats, great lyricism, and Psycho Les, JuJu, and Fashion (later known as Al' Tariq) embodied a confidence and laissez faire that I could only hope to emulate as a young, impressionable eighteen-year-old kid. Plus, they produced that Chi-Ali album a couple of years prior which was basically a demo tape of their beats. So this is my list...we would love to hear yours.

Joe November's Top Ten Native Tongues singles (in no particular order)

- "Listen 2 Me" - Queen Latifah (*Black Reign*)
- "Breakadawn" - De La Soul (*Buhloone Mind State*)
- "Oodles of O's" - De La Soul (*De La Soul is Dead*)
- "Trouble in the Water" - DJ Honda feat. De La Soul (*h II (Japan Edition)*)
- "Lyrics to Go" - A Tribe Called Quest (*Midnight Marauders*)
- "Vibes and Stuff" - A Tribe Called Quest (*The Low End Theory*)
- "Miscellaneous (Hi-Tek Luv Boat Mix)" - Phife Dawg (*Ventilation: Da LP*)
- "Non-Fiction Outro" - Black Sheep (*Non-Fiction*)
- "Butt in the Meantime" - Black Sheep (*A Wolf in Sheep's Clothing*)
- "Funky Lemonade (Beatnuts remix)" – Chi-Ali (*The Fabulous Chi-Ali*)

CHAPTER FIVE
PROFOUND'S LISTS

Profound's Top Ten Native Tongues Albums

- *Midnight Marauders* - A Tribe Called Quest (1993)
- *Stakes is High* - De La Soul (1996)
- *The Grind Date* - De La Soul (2004)
- *The Low End Theory* - A Tribe Called Quest (1991)
- *A Wolf in Sheep's Clothing* - Black Sheep (1991)
- *All Hail the Queen* - Queen Latifah (1989)
- *3 Feet High & Rising* - De La Soul (1989)
- *People's Instinctive Travels and the Paths of Rhythm* - A Tribe Called Quest (1990)
- *AOI Bionix* - De La Soul (2001)
- *Black Reign* - Queen Latifah (1993)

Profound's Top Ten Native Tongues Songs

- "Stakes is High" - De La Soul (*Stakes is High*)
- "The Bizness" - De La Soul feat. Common (*Stakes is High*)
- "Award Tour" - A Tribe Called Quest (*Midnight Marauders*)
- "Wrath of my Madness" - Queen Latifah (*All Hail the Queen*)
- "Rock Co.Kane Flow" - De La Soul feat. MF Doom (*The Grind Date*)

- "Check the Rhime" - A Tribe Called Quest (*The Low End Theory*)
- "U.N.I.T.Y." - Queen Latifah (*Black Reign*)
- "The Choice Is Yours" - Black Sheep (*A Wolf in Sheep's Clothing*)
- "Scenario" - A Tribe Called Quest (*The Low End Theory*)
- "Itzsoweezee" - De La Soul (*Stakes is High*)

Honorable mention:

- "Flavor of the Month" – Black Sheep
- "One Two Sh*t" – A Tribe Called Quest
- "Buddy (remix)" - De La Soul
- "Scenario (remix)" A Tribe Called Quest
- "Buggin' Out" – A Tribe called Quest

CHAPTER SIX
Beau Brown's Top 12 Favorite Phife Verses

He was a good emcee but never the best. His solo album(s)[1] were decent but nothing spectacular. He's well-known by every Hip-Hop head, but he didn't have the mainstream recognition of his closest partner in rhyme (Q-Tip). But there's something about Phife Dawg that I have always loved. Maybe it's the underdog appeal–only 5'3", diabetic, and self-deprecating, but confident and smooth nonetheless. Maybe it's the continual improvement I saw in him over his career. Maybe it's the way he spoke organically about politics and justice (not overbearing or forced). More likely, it's all of the above. Malik Taylor is a legendary artist, and he deserves to be in the highest echelons of Hip-Hop taxonomy.

With a relatively large body of work, it can be difficult to pinpoint a selection of Phife's verses that represent his conceptual and lyrical range. While Top 5 and Top 10 lists are fun to analyze and debate, I'm not sure I could come up with a rating system that would lend any credence to a list like this. Instead, what I decided to do is simply list my 12 favorite Phife Diggy verses, along with a brief rationale for each. My hope is that you'll have a different set of favorite verses (maybe some of which I haven't even heard) and let me know about them. Nonetheless, here's my contribution.

---

[1] Depending on how you slice it, you could argue that Phife only really had one solo album. Forever was never finished, even though I'm glad they went ahead and released it.

1. **"Buddy (Native Tongues Decision)" - De La Soul (1988)** - 18-year-old Phife Diggy makes his recorded debut with a smooth 8 bars sandwiched between Mike G (from the Jungle Brothers) and Q-Tip. I wish it was longer, but the verse is dope nonetheless.

2. **"Buggin' Out" (Verse 1) - A Tribe Called Quest (*The Low End Theory*, 1991)** - This has to be one of the best opening lines in Hip-Hop history. The way he comes in with "Yo…" feels so authoritative, and if you don't start bobbing your head when he says "microphone check one two, what is this?" I'd have to question whether your heart is still beating.

3. **"Check the Rhime" (Verse 2) - A Tribe Called Quest (*The Low End Theory*, 1991)** - In this funky introduction of how nice he is, the Five-Foot Assassin gives a middle finger to the punk emcees, and it's lovely.

4. **"Scenario" (Verse 1) - A Tribe Called Quest (*The Low End Theory*, 1991)** - I smile every time I hear him say "Bo don't know Jack, cuz Bo can't rap." Growing up with the name Beau (pronounced "Bo") right as Vincent "Bo" Jackson was breaking bats and rushing down the field as a Raider, this line immediately registered with me.

5. **"La Schmoove" - Fu-Schnickens (*F.U. Don't Take it Personal*, 1992)** - It may be true that Phife had "nothing to prove" after *The Low End Theory*, but he does it anyway. Displaying his versatility, both stylistically and content-wise, Phife kicks braggadocious rhymes with the promise that he has much more in store.

6. **"Stir It Up (Steve Biko)" (Verse 1) - A Tribe Called Quest (*Midnight Marauders*, 1993)** - There's that self-deprecating swagger he's famous for: "The height of Muggsy Bogues, complexion of a hockey puck." Mutty Ranks is proud of who he is, whether anyone else likes it or not.

7. **"Electric Relaxation" (Verse 2) - A Tribe Called Quest (*Midnight Marauders*, 1993)** - There's a reason one of his monikers was "Malik The 5-Foot Freak." Phife loved women (including his future wife), and this verse is clear evidence of that. Although he drops several gems as he goes back and forth with Q-Tip throughout the song, this verse sets the tone.

8. **"1nce Again" (Verse 1) - A Tribe Called Quest (*Beats, Rhymes and Life*, 1996)** - My favorite song from my favorite Tribe album. Phife comes hard with some battle raps here (*puttin' emcees to the test*), and he's definitely in his pocket.

9. **"Lemme Find Out" (Verse 1)" - Phife Dawg (*Ventilation: Da LP*, 2000)** - It was magic when Phife and Pete Rock connected. Phife just sounds hungry on this whole song. He's held it in so long, and I'm glad he finally let it out.

10. **"Peace, Prosperity, and Paper" (Verse 2) - A Tribe Called Quest (*Hits, Rarities & Remixes*, 2003)** - *Yeah, I wanna go gold, platinum, uh huh, etc, but why put out some wackness when no one will respect ya?* This is the level of introspection I love to hear from Phife. I'm not sure he ever converted to Islam, but you can tell Q-Tip and Ali were influencing him to think deeply about it.

11. **"Nutshell" (Verse 1) - Phife Dawg (2016)** - If we're talking about the whole song, "Nutshell Pt. 2" is better, since it comes with dope verses from Busta and Redman. However, Phife's first verse in the original is magnificent. *Undefeated, unblemished, underrated...* Brilliant poetic technique!

12. **"We the People" (Verse 2) - A Tribe Called Quest (*We Got It from Here…Thank You 4 Your Service*, 2016)** *Who can come back years later, still hit the shot?* Phife can! The few years leading up to his untimely death were such a productive time for him. I'm grateful he left us verses like this to remember him.

So, there's my "Best of Phife" mixtape. I hope it gives you a nice trip down memory lane or helps you discover a few dope verses for the first time. There will never be another rapper or human being like Phife Dawg. Rest in peace to one of the greats!

Part Two

Retrospectives & Reviews

CHAPTER SEVEN

Straight Out the Jungle
Jungle Brothers
Written by iomos marad

I remember it like it was yesterday! I was a young Black male going into the 10th grade who was very immature and unsure about what I would become in the future. As a matter of fact, there was little or no thought about what I would become in the near future because I was too busy playing in the present. Not only was I unsure about my future, but I had very low self-esteem about who I was as a young Black man. I also had some intuitive sense that I would face rejection by the people within my community who shared the same reflection as me as well as others outside of my community who didn't see any value in me because of the color of my skin.

    I also remember having a love-hate relationship with school even though I always seemed to thrive in classes where reading and writing were at the forefront. If I'm being honest, I was an A-B student performing at a C-D level. To put it plain, I would do just enough to get by but my "just getting by" mentality created tension between me and my mom because my mom knew the importance of education from her own lived experience. Another thing I hated about school was the social class structure around popularity that was created by the agents of capitalism and producers of the latest and greatest fashions that all urban Black youth embraced. Fashionable fabrics bearing known names of brands set the social parameters and pace of the culture of my school that I hated. In other words, I was not in the "in crowd" based on my wears. To this day, I have owned only two pairs of Jordans in my entire life. That should give you an idea of where I was at. Needless to say, it was a crazy time in my life. And during this time, I had not yet embraced who I am now as a Black man today, and I had not grasped the importance of education and how education can be used for a purpose.

SO LET ME SET THE SCENE FOR YOU...HERE I AM, a young Black male, with low self-esteem and worth, with no clue of what I wanted to be in life and thinking that I was predestined for rejection and failure based on the color of my skin. I was haunted by questions like:

Who am I? Where did I and my people come from? What will I be in the future? When will I become? How will I become? Will I become?

All these questions are circulating and racing through my mind as I'm walking around the corner to my cousin Leon's house from school. As I'm approaching the front door, I'm hearing this music and lyrics blasting out of all the open windows and screen doors of my cousin's house:

> *Educated Man / From the motherland / You see they call me a star but that's not what I am / Imma Jungle Brother/ A true blue brother / And I bet you many faces you'll Neva discover / Step to my side / Suckers run and hide / Afrika's in the house they get petrified / You wanna know why / I tell you why / Because they can't stand the sight of the jungle eye / They never fight or fuss / They never curse or cuss / They just stand on the side and stare at us / They get out of line / I put on a vine and give em one big push for all mankind / It ain't nothin to it / I just go*

'head and do it / Lay down the jungle sound and run right through it / And when I'm on the mic / I neva stutter or stumble / 'Cause Imma Jungle Brother / Straight out the jungle

Now inside, I just remember walking right toward the speakers in some type of trance as my cousin put the cassette tape in my hand, instinctively knowing that I would want to look at the artwork and read the liner notes. As I'm hearing this music and words pour out of the speakers, what I didn't know at the time is these specific lyrics belonged to Afrika Baby Bam who is the "frontman" of the legendary rap group, the Jungle Brothers. Then you had the smooth and laidback Mike G and DJ Sammy B to complete the three-man trio of Hip-Hop masters. To me, *Straight Out the Jungle* is one of the most important albums of Hip-Hop not only because the music is dope but because the content of the lyrics is still with me today. This is an album that I always find myself going back to no matter what.

I later discovered that the Jungle Brothers were one of the groups in the Afrocentric-centered collective known as the Native Tongues, consisting of the Jungle Brothers, A Tribe Called Quest, De La Soul, and others. These groups were and still are very influential not only in my development as an emcee/artist but in who I am and what I am pursuing in my life right now.

Anyway, the words of that song and the *Straight Out the Jungle* album have moved and shaped me in countless ways. It not only moved and shaped me, but it has answered all of my "Who Am I?" questions. I felt like Afrika was telling me at that moment that I am an educated Black man from the motherland known as Africa. This newfound consciousness and awareness: Knowledge of Self, gave me two things: (1) confidence in myself, and (2) a desire to find and use my voice to move others the same way that Afrika's lyrics moved me.

Straight Out the Jungle comes out the gate with straight conscious-centered messages, starting with the album title track to "What's Going On" and "Black is Black (Featuring Q-Tip)." Hearing "Black is Black" was my first introduction to Q-Tip and, after hearing him rhyme, I knew I wanted to be an emcee like him. I remember doing the verses to "Black is Black" at my school's assembly because my teacher heard me saying the J-Beez rhymes while beating on my desk in class during a break. I tried my best to hone in Mike G's energy beating on the table on stage while rhymin'

> *Now, history was not my favorite subject*
> *I used to flip through the pages and get upset*
> *Seein' little of black and too much of the other*
> *(They tried to brainwash you) Picture that, a Jungle Brother*
> *Read this, read that, answer question 3*
> *But when I got to 3, it had nothin' to do with me*
> *Somethin' was wrong, and I knew it all along*
> *Now tell me (please) what's goin' on*

The Jungle Brothers followed the trend of the time by speaking on the times of the day but making sure they didn't leave the ladies out with songs like "Jimbrowski", "I'm Gonna Do You", "I'll House You", and "Behind the Bush". I remember getting a girl's phone number at the mall reciting the lyrics of "I'm Gonna Do You" to this fine brown skinned honey. I hit her with "Girl. Ooh you look fine / I wanna do you." I didn't really know what "I'm gonna do you" meant at the time, but I got that number tho (laughing).

Then there were the braggadocious joints like "On the Run", "Because I Got It Like That", "Braggin and Boastin", and "The Promo" which features Q-Tip again coming with:

My bone is grabbed / this is what I mean / I brag and grab / and here's the scene / Q-Tip (Q-Tip) from A Tribe Called Quest / On the Jungle Brothers album (Oh yes) / So get the ducats / It's coming out soon / A month after March / two before June / It's nice with Ali Shaheed Muhammad / My DJ who is real dominant (Muhammad/ Muhammad)

He and I form the funky Tribe / If you want to get with it / just feel the vibe (Feel the vibe) / Me and Ali are extremely witty and / To be heard like the horn of Gideon

And to top it all off, they even left room for DJ Sammy B to get loose on "Sounds of The Safari" and "Jimmy's Bonus Beat." This album has everything for everyone, and if you have never heard this album before or if you have not listened to it in a while, I urge you to take a listen.

Straight Out the Jungle is a classic album that will forever be a part of my life. I don't think I would be where I am today if it wasn't for this album. I would like to thank you Afrika, Mike G, and Sammy B for creating a timeless piece of art for a brother like me to revisit and learn from until my time on this earth is done.

CHAPTER EIGHT

From The Soul Comes DA Inner Sound Y'all (DAISY):
De La Soul's *3 Feet High and Rising*

Written by Jason Cuthbert

One album arrived in 1989 that seemed to be created right when I needed it the most, after I had to step outside the comfort zone of Marvel comic books and G.I. Joe action figures and figure out that post-childhood thing with girls and stuff. It was called *3 Feet High and Rising*, a title that literally sounded like growing up from a little kid's stature, by De La Soul.

WHOA. It was like the colorful fun of my Kid 'n Play *2 Hype* tape, the vivid story tales of Slick Rick, the cultural pride of Public Enemy, and the poetic puzzles of Rakim—all for the price of one affordable trip to the mall. Plus, this De La Soul group looked as strange as I felt inside my awkward body. Sign me up!

You know those audio equivalents of *Saturday Night Live* skits on Hip-Hop albums that have given us memorable moments like The Mad Rapper player hating on The Notorious B.I.G.'s *Life After Death*, Ghostface Killah's fabulous instructions for changing the colorway of his suede Clarks Wallabees on Raekwon's *Only Built for Cuban Linx*, and Black Sheep's hilarious gangster rapper parody of waking up from a dream, stating "You mean I'm not...hard?" from *A Wolf in Sheep's Clothing?*

I enjoyed those and many other cinematic intros, outros, and interludes too. But before they became normal threads to string songs together on conceptual Hip-Hop albums, De La Soul invented the use of these rap-related "skits," which they initially referred to as "bug-out pieces" for *3 Feet High and Rising*. With several segments of a fictitious game show, they used an ingenious way to introduce us to the De La members and their zany sense of humor, while also accidentally flooding the desk of their Tommy Boy Records' A&R executive Dante Ross with mailed in answers to impossible questions, like "How many feathers are on a Perdue chicken?"[2]

There were also trippy album breaks with Martians that happen to speak French called "Transmitting Live from Mars" and the moans and groans of "De La Orgee" that my youthful virginity prevented me from understanding in 1989. In celebration of De La Soul's game-changing contribution to the world of music, I will share a few of my own "skits" in the form of personal memories of *3 Feet High and Rising*.

Inside Jokes for Outsiders

<u>Memory Skit 1</u>: When I first listened to the entire *3 Feet High and Rising* album all the way through, I don't recall it being in the headphones of my Sony Walkman or with the home stereo volume turned down really low to hide any sudden curse words from my parents. Instead, I was listening to the very first De La Soul album (and my first full-length experience of the Native Tongues collective) in the backseat of a car with my elementary school friend Aaron Medina as his dad drove us to Darien Lake, the best amusement park you could go to in under an hour from our city, Rochester, New York.

Thinking back, I remember how much we were all laughing and mimicking the lyrics and De La dialogue. It also helped that Aaron's dad was laid-back enough not to be bothered by the

---

[2] This information is out there, but for the life of us, we can't find the source. If you find it, let us know and we'll update future versions of the book.

album's random profanity and occasional sexual references in the lyrics. I was nervously waiting to see if Mr. Medina was going to yank the tape out of the cassette deck and unspool it into the trash (which I'm sure would have happened in my parent's car). But it never took place, so the coast was clear, and it was OK to just keep laughing and go with the flow.

Looking back on that time now, De La was never a mean-spirited crew anyway. The group's messages were positive enough for a kid back then to successfully graduate from "Rated PG to Rated PG-13" content relatively unscathed and brightly enlightened. De La's inside jokes and expressions would later become my inside jokes with other artsy outsiders and open minds that I cliqued up with that also held this band in high regard.

De La Soul's debut album *3 Feet High and Rising* is overflowing with hidden meanings for thoughtful listeners to decode and discover. Let's start with the group's name…De La Soul. How cool was it in 1989 for this African-American Hip-Hop group to have a name written predominantly in Spanish? Between me growing up with close friends that were Latino and me getting taught Spanish in elementary school, it wasn't hard for me to figure out that De La Soul meant "From the Soul", they even mentioned it on the album for those paying attention.

Now on to the individual names of the group members because those monikers had particular meanings too. The three members were referred to as "plugs," like microphone plugs. Plug 1 was the MC named Posdnous, which was "Sound Sop" spelled backward. There was a very good reason for that. Posdnous DJed under the name DJ Soundsop back in 1985 in an early local Long Island, New York group called Easy Street with his partner Trugoy, who beatboxed under his middle name "Jude" back then.[3]

---

[3] *Check the Technique* by Brian Coleman in the De La Soul chapter on making 3 Feet High and Rising on pages 144 and 145 of the paperback copy.

Speaking of Trugoy the Dove, on *3 Feet High and Rising*, he rapped as Plug 2, the MC whose name Trugoy was "yogurt" spelled backward in tribute to his favorite food at the time. Then there was Plug 3, De La Soul's DJ, recognized as "PA Mase" (as in a Public Address system) or Pasemaster Mase. Mase was a shortened version of his last name "Mason" and "MASE" stood for "Making A Soul Effort."

DE LA GLOSSARY

Buddy: a body that grabs your attention

Daisy Age: "DAISY" stands for Da Inner Sound Y'all, which was the music from their soul. De La Soul made it clear that they weren't passive hippies and apparently had to prove it by beating up wannabe bullies who got the De La image mixed up.

Dan Stuckie: anything referred to as awesome and amazing.

Jenny: vagina

Jimmy: penis

Public Speaker: a dope, skilled MC

Not Psychedelic…PsycheDeLa

Memory Skit 2: I remember in the late 2000s when I first saw the famous day-glow design for *3 Feet High and Rising* make its way onto shoes after De La Soul collaborated with Nike to produce two versions of the Nike Dunk sneakers under the Nike SB skateboarding division. I soon realized that I was going to have to buy those incredible yellow, green, and brown high-top De La Dunks online because they were obviously way too exclusive for traditional sneaker locations. What would transpire next made my jaw drop. I saw those De La Nikes being resold on eBay for well over $300. That might not sound like much money to current sneakerheads. But to me and my little 2006 disposable spending, that was insane. These, along with the coveted MF Doom Nike SB Dunks, would become two pairs of sneakers that got away and were above my pay grade.

The iconic De La album cover for *3 Feet High and Rising* pulled me right in because it felt like the first one I could have figured out how to accomplish myself, maybe with a black and white photocopy cut-out collage of the group and my yellow, pink, and green back-to-school shopping fluorescent highlighters. But the art direction was much more sophisticated, done by art director Toby Mott, from the rebellious British art collective The Grey Organization, with beginnings in the 1970s Punk movement who relocated to New York City.

De La's visual concept was executed by having De La Soul come to Grey Organization's NYC loft, lie down on the floor forming a triangle with their faces staring upwards, having their photo taken from up above on a step ladder, hand-drawn flower designs made with Posca paint pens on acetate over the photographic portrait print, that was then copied with a rostrum camera that was used normally in filmmaking and television to manually produce on-screen titles and artwork to film.[4]

De La Soul also had their own comic strip inside the printed album cover sleeve by Michael Uman, a New York-based art director, illustrator, animator, designer, and musician who worked in the art department of Russell Simmons' Rush Artist Management. The black and white sketches featured De La Soul

---

[4] https://www.theguardian.com/music/2014/apr/29/how-we-made-3-feet-high-and-rising-de-la-soul

traveling to Earth from Mars, where they are commissioned by a duck named "Dante the Scrubb" (an inside joke between De La and famed producer/ music executive Dante Ross) to fulfill the mission of completing the album *3 Feet High & Rising* with assistance from Jungle Brothers and Q-Tip.

With a hypnotic album cover that always looked right-side-up no matter which way you shifted it, comedy skits, exclusive comic book drawings, and the equivalent of two albums' worth of music, De La's debut felt like a total sensory adventure each time I replayed it. By the way, they were clearly onto something with the album cover for *3 Feet High and Rising* because it has been archived in the permanent collection of the MoMA (Museum of Modern Art) in Manhattan, New York.

Soundbites Without Biting

Memory Skit 3: I'm pretty sure the first time I ever listened to a Hip-Hop song and had the nostalgic feeling of recognizing its sampled sounds was when I noticed Eddie Murphy's voice from his "Hit By a Car" stand-up comedy routine on De La's song "The Magic Number." It's all because I had bought the 1982 *Eddie Murphy* comedy album years earlier when I was way too young to be hearing that cuss fest, years before Parental Advisory stickers were a thing. I carried that cassette with me to grade school, showing it off to kids in my class and afraid my parents would find it, hearing Eddie in raw form.

In the same way that De La Soul was ground-breaking in utilizing the Hip-Hop skit to conceptually tie an album together, they unfortunately had another alleged first, getting hit with massive lawsuits along with their record label Tommy Boy Records because of their masterful mix of sampling tidbits, including the infamous case over the 1969 song from The Turtles, "You Showed Me" on the De La skit, "Transmitting Live from Mars."

But in better news, in 2011, their every-genre-in-one Hip-Hop production style with producer Prince Paul (who went to the same high school as all the members in Amityville, New York) helped get *3 Feet High and Rising* chosen among 25 albums to get added to the Library of Congress' 2010 National Recording Registry for cultural, esthetical, and historical impact. Steely Dan's album Aja was also named to the registry that year, which was ironically sampled on *3 Feet High and Rising*. Even the title of the album came from a vocal sample of singer Johnny Cash on "The Magic Number," the same track that pulls from the dreamy backing music from the *Schoolhouse Rock* educational cartoons (no 'sample snitching' over here, this is public record).

According to the De La Soul electronic press kit for *3 Feet High and Rising,* they fused the eclectic music collections of their parents for their naturally different sounds: Jazz from Plug 1's parents, some more Jazz, Country, and Reggae from Plug 2's parents, and a little bit of Calypso and R&B from the mom and pops of Plug 3.

Take that Jheri Curl Off

Memory Skit 4: When I finally was able to find and buy my own faux leather African medallion necklace at the end of the 1980s (which I still have), in an era when the news of the horrors of apartheid in South Africa didn't need non-existent social media to reach our awareness in North America, I was inspired by Pro-Black artists like Public Enemy, Spike Lee, and most certainly De La Soul. Along with their Native Tongues brothers and sisters, De La took the stance to wear Afrocentric jewelry instead of the opulent gold chains that still remain as rapper status symbols to this day. I wish I could have gotten my hands on one of those custom De La Soul medallions they wore in music videos as well, which I would be willing to pay for right this very second. With most of my clothing at that point consisting of sports teams and t-shirts with pop-culture graphics, this was one of the first times where Hip-Hop made me want to seek and represent a side of who I was through fashion that was outside of the norm.

De La Soul took a stand with their style on *3 Feet High and Rising*. Instead of begging people to accept their outcast outfits, they confidently went the other way and simply laughed at whoever was stuck in the aging, recycled 80s Hip-Hop uniform. On tracks like "Take it Off" and the "Me, Myself, and I" music video, De La Soul roasted copycats playing dress-up with humor that didn't make it safe out there for those that were too sensitive to take a joke about their Adidas shell-toes with fat laces, color contact lenses, mock-neck Le Tigre long sleeves with bomber coats, Kangol caps with juicy jheri curls underneath, and Jordache jeans.

In 1989, De La Soul preferred baggy Girbaud denim, casual plaid, paisley, and striped shirts, Afro-centric dashikis, earth tones, pants not jeans, shoes not sneakers, natural dreadlocks and slanted high-tops, and of course, "African, medallions, no gold." Trugoy said it in "Me, Myself, and I":

> *Style is surely our own thing. Not the false disguise of showbiz.*

In a 2009 interview with *Rolling Stone,* Trugoy further stated:

> We felt like, if we wanted to look the way we looked and touch on topics we did, we shouldn't be fearful of doing it just because it was the boasting and the bragging and the gold chain era. We always felt that individualism and creativity and expressing it was most important.

And while you are at it, take the immortal advice of De La producer and one half of the Handsome Boy Modeling School, Prince Paul (Stetsasonic's DJ since the 10th grade):

Take those acid-washed jeans, bell-bottomed, designed by your mama...Off? Please? Please?

A Phrase Called "Talk"

Memory Skit 5: On the highly imaginative track "Tread Water," De La Soul tells multiple short stories, teaching the morals of having compassion, never giving up, and overcoming fears. What made this song seem like an after-school cartoon that I would run home to watch was the hallucinogenic details that mirror Sesame Street characters during an acid trip. These guys were fearless, having written a rap song about a talking squirrel, monkey, and crocodile that never gets old. But when Posdnous rapped about Mr. Fish chatting with him from his bathroom sink, I couldn't help but rewind my mind in time to a children's picture book I used to love called *A Fish Out of Water,* about Otto, an orange goldfish that a little boy overfeeds and causes to grow too big for the house. It was based on a Dr. Seuss story, and my mother used to read it to me before bed. De La Soul was able to tap into my youngest years, teaching me that words can resurrect priceless memories and conjure vivid daydreams for the audience, proving it's alright to be a fish out of water instead of drowning in a shark tank of hardcore macho attitudes.

In the world of *3 Feet High and Rising,* "Potholes in My Lawn" was about rappers trying to steal their lyrical style; the "lawn" was the pages of their written lyrics, and the "potholes" were the missing pieces of poetry. "Ghetto Thang" really touched my heart with its explanation of how neighborhoods crippled by poverty can create trauma, teen parenthood, deadly violence, and shattered dreams, just like the streets where some of my friends and classmates lived that had it way worse than me.

"Say No Go" was the kind of catchy anti-drug song that made me never want to even try smoking crack or be anywhere near it;

the kind of message I wish kids of the 2020s had more mainstream access to. "Eye Know" was that super cool love song that made sex a secondary priority to compatible companionship.

If there is one massive transformative thing that I owe to De La Soul's *3 Feet High and Rising,* it is how it really taught me the importance of reading between the lines of any information that is presented to me. It exercised my mind muscles to translate their clever lyrics that were layered with multiple meanings, pop culture references, and contemporary Shakespeare-level phrases that I refused to let fly right over my head. It was the first album in Hip-Hop, or any genre of music for that matter, that rewarded me with dozens of new hidden Easter eggs of information the more that I listened to it. Also, with 24 tracks, the longest Hip Hop album I ever owned up until that point, there was over an hour worth of art to revisit and understand while improving my vocabulary immensely in the process.

I have to admit, *3 Feet High and Rising* made me really appreciate creative writing, to the point of wanting to challenge myself to be more honest in my self-expression, even when people don't get my vision. Before *3 Feet High and Rising,* I didn't realize that you could be funny, serious, surreal, cerebral, modern, retro, timeless, and the inventor of your own words, all in the same project if you wanted to. Like all fine art, De La Soul made me keep asking questions about what they created and find the answers on my own. From 1989 to 2000-Now, De La Soul is an inspiration to grant myself the creative license to drive my ideas forward to make meaningful statements and steer my own imagination in the direction of being true to who I am.

CHAPTER NINE

All Hail the Queen
Queen Latifah
Written by Donald "Profound" DeVold

I first became aware of Queen Latifah from her single "Ladies First." I was a sophomore in high school and having just received Alex Haley's *Autobiography of Malcolm X* for Christmas that year I was immediately attracted to the persona that is Queen Latifah. Back in 1989 there was a surge in what could be identified as The Conscious Era of Hip-Hop. During that summer Public Enemy released "Fight the Power", a single from the Spike Lee movie "Do the Right Thing." Also that same year was Boogie Down Productions' *Ghetto Music: The Blueprint of Hip-Hop* with the singles "Why is That?" and "You Must Learn." Both songs brought consciousness to the forefront of the Hip-Hop movement. Add the Native Tongues and Queen Latifah to the scene and it was pure magic.

    The Queen's first album *All Hail the Queen* was the perfect introduction to who Queen Latifah was as an artist. What was unique about this time was that Hip-Hop music had a huge dance element. There were dancers (B-boys, B-girls, etc.) for just about every Hip-Hop artist, be it a group or solo. *All Hail the Queen* starts off with "Dance for Me", an up-tempo Hip-Hop dance song that was backed by a video as well. Dressed in a military uniform the Queen takes court. The song is positive, fun, and it will make you move as you can hear Mark "The 45" King's sound on the production. The 2nd song "Mama Gave Birth to the Soul Children" features Native Tongues members De La Soul. What I notice most about this song is everybody sounds like they belong. Plus, the samples used sound like something from *3 Feet High and Rising.* This is a perfect mesh of the Queen and De La. I can see why the Native Tongues were all fond of each other. You can feel the camaraderie within the crew as Queen Latifah still shines throughout. With features from De La Soul, Monie-Love, and KRS-ONE this was a genius way to release her first project.

I still remember the "pulse" of Hip-Hop back then. I was so enamored about learning new things, learning about my ethnicity, and having the feeling of pride that I was SOMEBODY. Then here comes Queen Latifah teaching me what my mother was already instilling in me: to respect women and never treat them as lesser. With stand-out songs "Dance for Me", "Mama Gave Birth to the Soul Children", "Ladies First", "Wrath of my Madness", "Queen of Royal Badness", and "Evil That Men Do", this was most definitely a top Hip-Hop release in 1989. Latifah hits all marks of an emcee. Yes, I said emcee not female emcee. Her contribution to Hip-Hop and the Native Tongues is undeniable, so much so Dana Owens is still referred to as "Queen."

*Profound's original reflection of *All Hail the Queen* can be found in *The Boom Bap Review Volume 3: 2021*

CHAPTER TEN

People's Instinctive Travels and the Paths of Rhythm
A Tribe Called Quest
Written by Donald "Profound" DeVold

April 1990: I was a sophomore in high school when A Tribe Called Quest released their first album. I remember being so excited to get it. I was an unemployed 15-year-old desperately begging my parents to buy this album for me. Of course, they didn't. Luckily, I was cool with all the neighborhood DJs and was able to get a copy. Being familiar with ATCQ from the De La Soul "Buddy" remix and from their own single "I Left My Wallet in El Segundo", I couldn't wait to put it on. When I think back to listening to this album for the first time, I never thought about listening to it 30 years later and still sounding as fresh as it did back then. There was a plethora of classic Hip-Hop albums released that year and, looking back, I know why this album grabbed my attention so much. The production was stellar. The sample choices and drum-breaks were different from what I was used to hearing. The rhymes were clever, smooth, and intellectual but fun. "Bonita Applebum", the 2nd single released from this album, is laced with a smooth laid-back loop (Ramp's "Daylight") playing the background underneath hard boom bap drums. This song became an instant hit at all the parties. You can still feel the energy when any DJ plays it as the intro starts:

> *Do I love you; Do I lust for you? Am I a sinner because I do the two?*

Q-Tip playfully teases in the beginning before the main groove drops and you get mesmerized.

Bonita Applebum, ya gotta put me on, Bonita Applebum, I said ya gotta put me on.

You can do nothing but nod your head to this song. A Tribe Called Quest chose to be themselves and not follow the norm. This was evident on "Bonita Applebum" as well as other standout songs like "Push it Along", "Luck of Lucien", "Footprints", "Can I Kick It?", "Youthful Expressions", and more. That's what makes ATCQ great. They did it their way with great influential and positive music. Here I am, 32 years later writing a reflection about a group that I truly admire. I didn't really know the significance of ATCQ back then. I'm sure most people didn't. I'm just glad to be able to write about them now and appreciate the dope music they've given us. Have you ever heard ATCQ's first album *People's Instinctive Travels and the Paths of Rhythm*? If not, I'm happy to introduce you to it through this reflection. Peace.

CHAPTER ELEVEN

Down to Earth
Monie Love

Written by MC Till

Monie in the middle" sets it off just right. The upbeat drums with light conga hits give the rhythm a little something extra. The funky horns during the verse reside during the hook as sparkling organ hits accent the "Monie in the Middle" refrain. Lyrically it is a great song of empowerment where Monie Love is being pursued by an uninvited suitor. She is not playing any games and she lets him know without faltering. This upbeat, confident song is a great entry into what is about to be an enjoyable ride. Let's go.

"It's a Shame" is a great song to place next. It is not my favorite song on the album but definitely the most influential. I remember watching this video as a kid and being enthralled by her lyrical aptitude. I obviously didn't use this kind of word back then because I was fairly young. I did not get the message of the song either. It was not the content that captured me. It was the music and her delivery. She was so fresh with lines like, *That's it, pack it up. Be wise my sister cause the facts keep stacking up. Tell him to kiss the you know what. Make sure the door is shut behind you. I do believe the brother's out of luck.* On paper, those lines may not look incredible, but the way she dances around the rhythm with her voice is amazing. Also to note, these lines come in just after a bright saxophone solo. The music is deeply rooted with the voice, message, and delivery of Monie Love, creating a brilliant sound.

Okay, now we enter one of my favorite joints on the album with "Don't Funk Wid the Mo." This beat as well as over half the beats on the album are credited to Afrika Baby Bambaataa from the Jungle Brothers. Their sophomore album (and my favorite from them), *Done by the Forces of Nature* is funky and upbeat. That vibe is carried on here with this "Don't Funk Wid the Mo" track. The beat immediately reaches out and grabs my neck. I am forced to nod my head back and forth. This kind of feeling revisits us again and again on *Down to Earth*. I find myself snapping my neck on the Afrika Baby Bam-produced joints, specifically "R U Single", "Just Don't Give a Damn", "Down to Earth", and "Swiney Swiney". Baby Bam blends together funk, moments of disco vibes, intoxicating drum patterns, and groovy bass lines to formulate powerful landscapes for Monie Love to dazzle us with her delivery and uplifting messages.

Not only does Baby Bam provide funky beats. He also gives us a glimpse into what would become the driving sample behind the Black Sheep single "Strobelight Honey." On "Read Between the Lines", you hear this sample in the hook. It is super subtle. I'm not sure if Mista Lawnge heard it and was inspired to use it or if he heard it regardless of this Baby Bam beat. Either way, it is fun to listen to as an avid Native Tongues head. Speaking of fun and Native Tongues, the Beatnuts drop by to produce the beat for "Pups Lickin Bone", which features the same Baby Huey sample used on a "Can I Kick It" remix and one of my favorite Wu joints, "Buck 50" by Ghostface, Method Man, Cappadonna, and Redman. So that's cool.

Monie Love opens up this album funky and confident. She is in charge and lets it be known. That confidence holds strong throughout the duration of *Down to Earth*. It also holds true over 30 years later as this album remains one of the most succinct Native Tongues offerings. Monie is magnificent on the mic. She gives us a wealth of content to digest and does so in the most effortless way. She is fun, moving, and thought-provoking. She does all this over stellar production. *Down to Earth* is an often-overlooked album in a deep Native Tongues catalog. And to quote Monie Love, "It's a shame."

CHAPTER TWELVE

De La Soul is Dead
De La Soul

Written by MC Till

I might have cried. I definitely was angry and a bit sad. My body was all mixed up into one big bundle of negativity. Why? Because my older brothers and my dad got to stay up late and watch an important football game and I had to go to bed. I remember my mom[5] telling me to go upstairs. I don't remember if I stomped up those stairs or not, but I definitely had some pent-up emotion when I finally arrived in my room. It wasn't long before that pent-up anger diffused. That anger resting inside my 11-year-old body was quickly replaced by permeating "Oodles of O's", a story about "Bitties in the BK Lounge", and excursions into the wild world of *De La Soul is Dead*.

De La Soul's first album *3 Feet High & Rising* was an experience like no other. Nobody rapped like Pos and Dave. Nobody made albums like that. Samples were flying all around from every direction. Skits were trailing darn near every song. Skits were songs. Songs were skits. What was happening? You just got lost in it all, and that was okay because you didn't want to find your way out. You wanted to stay forever. All good things come to an end, I suppose, but even though De La Soul's sophomore album referenced their death, its experimental method of music was alive

---

[5] To be clear, my mom bought me the De La Soul is Dead tape a few weeks earlier, so she is the best.

and well. In many ways, their sophomore album was an extension of their debut with more off-kilter rhymes and even more skits. The experience continued. The only difference was that the music got better, if that's even possible!

Prince Paul and De La Soul kept all the fun elements of the debut but with more focus. *De La Soul is Dead* features a long-running story via skits throughout. A young bully provides scathing criticism of the group. The self-deprecating humor is lovely. The album's insert comes with a comic-book-style fold out so that the listener can read along. The album even features the words, "when you hear this sound, turn to the next page." Really, it's more like go to the next panel, but you get the idea. This is well-thought-out entertainment that is best experienced with one's full attention (it had all my attention that night in my room as the rest of my family watched the football game).

The skits are focused, but in a new, fresh way, and the music hits a tad differently this go around. The beats are harder. Drums are fuller. Beats for songs like "Oodles of O's", "Pease Porridge", "Let, Let Me In", "Millie Pulled a Pistol on Santa", and others pack a little more boom and bap than most of the beats on their debut album. Lyrically, Trugoy the Dove (Dave) and Posdnous are once again magnificent. As on their debut, they are witty and continue to find unique ways to deliver their rhymes. Listen to the stuttering, repeating effect they display on "Pease Porridge." Innovativeness and originality don't quite capture it. They were otherworldly, painting pictures by using brush strokes not yet invented.

The music is definitely on point and arguably better than *3 Feet High & Rising*. Perhaps more impressive was their spirit to keep the music pure. Their debut album blew up in a way nobody imagined. They felt forced into writing a radio-friendly hit, "Me, Myself, & I" (which they have been known to perform while saying "We hate this song.") They went with Tommy Boy's direction to highlight the daisy-laced psychedelic look. They got intro sampling trouble (well, to be fair, their label got into sampling trouble). So what did they do with their sophomore album? They announced they were dead in the title. They sampled probably just as much if not more. They released a single essentially bashing people for giving them their demo tapes. They beat out their own path, again.

De La Soul is De La Soul. They are as uncompromising as they come. Their legacy is a mix of incredible, timeless music and unparalleled influence. Before De La Soul, I got into LL Cool J and Biz Markie and the Beastie Boys, etc... I thought Hip-Hop music was cool. I had fun listening to it. After De La Soul entered the equation, my response to the music was different. Their music was not just good. It was an open invitation. It felt like they were speaking directly to me. Their music seemed to know my name. It understood my unquenchable desire to create something unique before I even knew that desire existed.

I met Dave (Trugoy the Dove) once in Atlanta. I was sitting in the food court at a mall. I don't remember which one. I see this man walking in the distance. He looked familiar. I tapped my friend and said, "I think that's the dude from De La Soul!" It was. I approached him, reached out my hand and said, "Just want to tell you how much your music means to me." He met my hand with his, looked me in the eye and said, "Thanks."

I was just one random dude in the mall, but there are countless people like me out there. De La Soul has affected many of us. Their music has encouraged us to appreciate art differently. They are pioneers. Together with Prince Paul, they crafted experiences with their albums. These experiences touched our lives, gave many of us permission to be ourselves. And for this emcee and beat maker, it gave me the inspiration I needed to go from a fan of the music to a participant.

Thank you, De La Soul. And thanks mom for sending me to my room early that night. It was one of the best nights I ever had.

CHAPTER THIRTEEN

The Low End Theory
A Tribe Called Quest

Written by MC Till

As De La Soul was following up their magnificent debut with a sophomore banger, A Tribe Called Quest was doing the exact same thing. De La dropped in May of 1991. Four months later in September, A Tribe Called Quest released one of the most monumental albums in Hip-hop, *The Low End Theory*. Whereas *De La Soul is Dead* clocked in at over 70 minutes and 27 tracks, *The Low End Theory* didn't reach 50 minutes with just 14 tracks. But don't let the length fool you. De La Soul went for a truly unique experience by blending skits and song. Tribe took a different approach. They crafted an album that's all about the music.

The very first sound on *The Low End Theory* is that of a standup bass. Ten seconds later, Q-Tip appears and, 20 seconds after that, the beat drops. This might be one of the greatest beginnings to any album ever. The bass line alone tells a story. It is something familiar. It is warm and inviting. Q-Tips follows in that same vein. Before the drums hit, his voice provides percussive vibes. It sits on top of that bass in such a beautiful way. If the listener is not hooked yet, the drums land and there is no escape. The rest of the song is pure delight. It also features perfectly placed horn samples. They are not loud but loud enough. Everything sounds so dope together. After the second verse, the horns return quickly before these new "Excursions" in sound fade.

If the beginning of "Excursions" is the greatest beginning to any song, the song itself might be the greatest beginning of any album. This first song is the catalyst for what is in store. The entire album features the perfect combination of standup bass, breakbeats, and jazzy samples. Phife and Q-Tip are exactly what they need to be on this album. They are witty at times. They tell stories. But, more than anything else, their presence is what's most important. Going back to *De La Soul is Dead*, Posdnous and Dave bring innovative deliveries along with inside-jokes-type-of-content. It is quirky. Phife and Tip, on the other hand, are much more straightforward. Pos and Dave are excelling in the creative writing class with extra credit points for being innovative while Tip and Phife are ditching class and just hanging out with their friends trading stories and rhymes. It is more approachable in a way. It is more centered around the accessible and universal language of music.

When I first heard this album at 11 years old, I didn't have the words to describe it. But I remember how I felt: engulfed. I couldn't stop listening to it. One song in particular really grabbed me. "Show Bizness" featured verses from Lord Jamar, Sadat-X, and Diamond D. I was a huge Brand Nubian fan at the time, and all these different emcees with their different styles and voices just mesmerized me. Another song that stood out was "What?" Remember when I said Phife and Tip cut class to go hang out? That's what this song feels like. It's like I'm there with Q-Tip, and he's just going off about all these different 'what' questions. It isn't anything super deep, but it is enchanting. Of course, two of their more popular singles, "Check the Rhime" and "Jazz (We've Got)", are super dope. Both of those songs are incredible in two different ways, and both had great videos to boot. Oh, and "Scenario" is arguably the greatest posse cut of all time. The beat is great. Each emcee brings great energy. It catapulted Busta Rhymes to another level. And it had a really fun video.

You know how I just got excited about a few songs from the album? Well, that's every song. I could jump into every song and share how much I love it. This album doesn't have a bad song. Some albums definitely have songs that are better than others. That's not really true here. All of the songs are great together. The album flows from greatness to greatness without missing a beat.

If you listen to the very last few seconds of *The Low End Theory,* you hear the words "So what's, so what's, so what's the scenario?" To find the answer to this final question, one only has to hit repeat. The scenario is a dedication to music. Q-Tip and Ali Shaheed Muhammad (with Skef Anslem being credited for working on two beats) brought together just the right blend of breakbeats, bass lines, and jazzy samples. Then the two emcees ensured that the music remained the focus. They stayed in the pocket. Or I guess I should say they stayed on that park bench with their friends. They joined the simple yet profoundly dope musical formula as their voices became the final instrument.

CHAPTER FOURTEEN

A Wolf in Sheep's Clothing Wrapped in a Conundrum
Black Sheep
Written by MC Till

My mom was an integral part of my love for and participation in Hip-Hop. The music wasn't her particular thing, but she was always supportive. I guess if she cut off Hip-Hop from me, perhaps that would have stirred a rebellious spirit that could have inspired me to get even more into it. Instead, she was supportive, and that helped me develop a healthy relationship with music. My dad was the same, too. They helped me become an active listener. One of my favorite songs on *A Wolf in Sheep's Clothing* is "To Whom it May Concern." Probably not a song an 11-year-old should play in front of their mom. But I was naive and innocent. Mister Lawnge refers to a woman getting a pap smear during his first verse. I had no idea what that was. My mom certainly did. She sat down and asked me if I knew what that meant. Then, she explained it to me. Can you imagine!?

    She let me listen to Black Sheep, and I'm so thankful she did. This album, *A Wolf in Sheep's Clothing*, is a masterpiece. It is one of my favorite albums of all time. Yet, some lyrics and songs on the album give me pause as an adult. They come across as misogynistic and crass to me. As a kid, many references went over my head. Others made me think twice, but I was pretty young and did not have the moral convictions to think a third time. Today, when I revisit this album and so many other albums, old or new, I have to face contradictions. I love this album. I mean I LOVE IT. At the same time, I don't like some of the lyrics. I guess it's not that I don't like the lyrics. It's that some of the lyrics stand in direct contrast to what is so beautiful about this album. Let's start there.

Dres is phenomenal, and his cadence is undeniable. No one utilizes inflection in such a prolific way. Well, maybe Scarface. Yeah, I'd say Scarface is the best at it, but Dres is not far behind. It is sometimes subtle, but Dres uses intonation to bring so much style to every verse. After the intro song ("U Mean I'm Not") that follows the actual intro, his first lines on the album are, "*It's times like this that I gotta crack a smile. If it's about anything, then it's gotta be style.*" Nothing really profound here. Not on paper. But when you listen to how he delivers these lines, he is exactly right. It is about style. The way he rhymes each line is entertaining. He writes verses that could contain hooks within them. You know that part of the verse where the emcee says something extra slick or engaging? The part that you remember each time? His verses are full of these moments. His vocal presence on this album is nothing less than spectacular.

Because Dres is so good on the mic, it would take some incredible production to keep up. Well, Mista Lawnge is down for the challenge. He provides over an hour of head nodding music, equipped with perfectly fitted breakbeats, samples that soar, and intoxicating bass lines. If Dres raised the bar lyrically, Mista Lawnge's beats matched it.

These seminal expressions of rhyme and beat come together in perfect form toward the very end of the album. Just before the album concludes, we get "The Choice is Yours (Revisited)." If not the best song in Hip-Hop, it must be considered as one of the best. It completes the album in firework form. All the tracks leading up to it are great. They dazzle the listener with bright lights and booming sounds. But "The Choice is Yours (Revisited)" is the grand finale. You know where it comes to a head, right? Yup! Just listen in at the 2:22 mark. The drums drop out, and Dres begins a new third verse, "*Engine, engine #9... Pick it up, pick it up, pick it up.*" Then that snare hits just as he says, "Back on the scene," and everyone in the place erupts.

So the music is exceptional. No question about it. As exceptional as it is, some of the lyrics referencing women on this album make me squirm. Again, when I was younger, I did not spend much time analyzing the context and implications of the lyrics. I just loved how the album felt. But I'm much older now, and when I hear certain lyrics today, I pause. How can I enjoy something so much that has sentiments that I don't share? There is definitely a line. I mean, I don't have to agree with everything an artist says. Far from it. I can enjoy music that conveys messages that I disagree with vehemently. Further, context is important. Art is often a reflection of reality, and reality is necessary even if unsettling.

Additionally, artists do grow. Often, this growth is reflected in their music. Common is a great example. He made a homophobic reference on a De La Soul song back in 1996. He often rapped lyrics referencing women in a similar way as I hear on this Black Sheep album. You don't hear Common in this light anymore. I believe this is due to the fact that he has grown as a person. He has learned. He has become a better version of himself. His reality has changed. I think the same is true with Dres. After Black Sheep's second album, you don't hear Dres rapping in the same way. I believe he has grown too, and his music reflects that growth. That kind of growth is something we can all aspire to, but we all have to start somewhere.

I also want to pause here and ensure that Dres (if you are reading) does not feel singled out. I mean, there are albums from that early 90s era with lyrics that were extremely misogynistic and inappropriate. There are albums that I personally cover in our annual *Boom Bap Reviews* that have lyrics far more problematic, including references to murder for no good reason. So why am I critiquing this particular album and this particular emcee? Well, hopefully if you read the previous two retrospectives or if you checked out the retrospective piece I did for *3 Feet High & Rising* in *The Boom Bap Review Volume 1*, then you might understand that these albums are much more than dope music to me. These albums and the Native Tongues in general influenced and inspired me more than any other group or artistic expression. The Native Tongues and their early albums were parts of my development not just as an artist myself but as a person. Yes, I could critique *Death Certificate* or *Quik is the Name* or any number of albums like I'm doing here with *A Wolf...*, but those albums are not the same. Those artists, although I admire them and listen to them, did not have the same profound effect on me like Dres and Black Sheep. I feel a more intimate relationship with *A Wolf in Sheep's Clothing*, so I feel a greater responsibility to the music and to be open and honest with how I feel about it.

Today, I couldn't be more excited that Dres is releasing new music. The songs and snippets I've heard are incredible and reflect a more mature Dres. This is in line with his solo work over the years. To me, Dres's work after the first two Black Sheep albums is much more thoughtful when it comes to lyrical content toward women. The evolution of Dres in this regard, I think, reflects a larger evolution within American culture. We can see a population grappling with hundreds of years of a male-centric society. #metoo, #believewomen, and other such hashtags reflect this change in culture.

I also saw it recently in sports commentary. When I was growing up watching ESPN and other networks in the mid 90s, I hardly ever saw a female sportscaster. I honestly don't remember seeing any. Well, when the Cincinnati Bengals made it to the Super Bowl this year, I decided to plug in and check out what the sports pundits were saying since I live in Cincinnati. I was pleasantly surprised to see the diversity. Women were present on pretty much every show I pulled up on YouTube, telling the audience about Joe Burrow this or Jamar Chase that. It was beautiful to see the difference from today's leadership of women vs yesteryear's non-presence. Perhaps the old guard is changing. Hopefully.

This is probably the most exciting thing for me as I reflect back on Dres and his career. In some ways, artistically, Dres is part of an old guard. He was there with the Native Tongues co-creating and influencing culture. But he is also a changing, evolving guard. He gave us some lyrics and skits that I personally find challenging like so many lyrics in so many Hip-Hop albums I love. He also gave us a classic album in *A Wolf in Sheep's Clothing*. Regardless of what I might think of certain lyrics, it is an incredible album with a top-notch lyrical performance and beats to match. Wrapped up in all this greatness is a reminder that music is never the final destination. It has to evolve. It has to grow. It has to get better. I think Dres is a great example while my mom is also a great example of someone who can help us wrestle with how we as listeners can participate in that progression.

CHAPTER FIFTEEN

Midnight Marauders Part 1
A Tribe Called Quest

Written by iomos marad

IOMOS MARAD'S PERSONAL REFLECTION OF MIDNIGHT MARAUDERS... AT THE MOMENT

Midnight Marauders and *Things Fall Apart* by the Roots are the two albums in my life where I felt like I could not move away from listening to them, even when new music was being released. It was something about those albums that would not allow me to go on with my life. I remember hanging out with my brother Bamski and him asking me, "What are you listening to?" And I excitedly replied, "I'm still on *Things Fall Apart*. To which he responded, "You still listen to that? You need to get on something new." But for whatever reason, I couldn't. And it was the same exact thing with *Midnight Marauders*. It was something about that album that just wouldn't let me go listen to other things.

9am (before lunch break)
Downtown Chicago, November 9, 1993

I'm working at a temp job as a file clerk for the Department of Children and Family Services. I can't stay focused on the job at hand because I know that *Midnight Marauders* is coming out today and the record stores don't open until 10am and I can't go on my lunch break until 12 or 1. Will there be any left? Can I get a poster? Will this album be better than *Low End Theory*? How can Tribe ever outdo *Low End*?

1pm (after lunch break analyzing the cover)

I'm back at my workspace just staring at the cover of the cassette tape, reading the liner notes (yes, I was still on cassettes back then). I didn't even go get food first. I went straight to the record store on my lunch break. I just grabbed some food that was closest to the record store with the time that I had left. Once I got back to the office and sat back down at my workstation, I just kept thinking to myself, "I can't believe how dope this album cover is." How did they do this? Yo! They got De La Soul and Jungle Brothers on here. Not to mention they put Hip-Hop generations with each other by positioning the artists together on the cover: from Zulu Nation members Afrika Bambaataa, Red Alert, Jazzy Jay to Grandmaster Flash and Crazy Legs (Rock Steady Crew) to Doug E. Fresh, Kool Moe Dee to MC Lyte, Special Ed, Heavy D, Daddy-O, and Chuck D, to the Pharcyde, Hieroglyphics, Del the Funky Homosapien, Souls of Mischief and Casual to Black Moon and even Sean Puffy Combs made an appearance on the cover before he became P. Diddy. Yo! This album cover is nuts.

1:30 or 1:45pm (The Listen)

After analyzing the album cover for 30 to 45 minutes, I finally pop the cassette into my walkman. As soon as I press play, I hear *errrup—errrup–errrup–errrup—hello* (at the same time this melodic, elevator type music with heavy strings starts going in the background while the female voice continues to talk) *this is your midnight marauder program. I'm on the front of your cover* (which made me instantly look at the cover again as if she was really a human being talking to me). *I will be enhancing your cassettes* (that's me, joe) *and CDs with certain facts that you may* *find beneficial (errrup—errrup—*Elevator music starts back again as the program continues to talk*) The average bounce meter for your midnight marauder program will be in the area of 95 BPMs. We hope that you will find our presentation precise. Bass heavy. And just right—Thanks.* And then—without any warning—these horns start blaring out of my headphones into my ears that catch me by surprise (I look around to see if anybody saw me jumping back in my seat). As the horns continue to blow, I hear my brother Phife Dawg come in with:

> *Linden Boulevard represent—represent (sent)/ Tribe Called Quest represent—represent (sent)/ When the mic is my hand I'm never hesitant/ My favorite jam back in the day was Eric B for presi—*

After hearing this intro, I had to rewind the tape back just so I could hear the start of "Steve Biko (Stir It Up)" again. I must have rewound that part at least 20 times. The horns, the drums, the *wow* of the guitar driving the song and the precise delivery of lyrics as only true emcees can do it. This Phife was not the Phife from *Low End Theory*; he came a looooong way from where he started on Tribe's debut album, breathin' lines like:

> *Hip-Hop scholar since being knee high to a duck/ The height of Muggsy Bogues/ complexion of a hockey puck/ You better ask somebody on how we flip the script/ Come to a Tribe show and watch the three kids rip*

Phife sets the pace of the song for Q-Tip to let his presence be felt with:

> *Queens is in the house represent, represent (sent)/ A Tribe Called Quest represent, represent (sent)/ No taming of the style 'cause it gets irreverent/ A Tribe Called Quest represent, represent (sent)/ Huh-huh,*

here we go, you know that I'm the rebel/ Throwing out the wicked like God did the Devil

Just imagine me trying to keep my composure in a downtown Chicago office space listening to Phife and Q-Tip *stir it up* on this song. I was sitting there with my hand over my mouth staring at the ceiling, saying to myself, "No these dudes didn't just set off an album like this. What the *expletive*." Only to hear one of the greatest pass-the-mic—set ups of all time by Phife to Q-Tip:

I just like to rhyme, kick the lyric skills like Pelé/ Tip educate 'em, my rhymes are strictly taboo / Fill 'em with some fantasies, and I'll look out like Tattoo Okay—IamrecognizingthatthevoiceinsidemyheadlsurgingmetobemyselfbutneverfollowsomeoneelseBecauseopinionsarelikevoicesweallhaveadifferentkindSojustcleanoutallofyourearsthesearemyviewsandyouwillfind—Thatwerevolutionizeoverthekick and the snare

I was stuck after hearing Q-Tip run off his first lines like that. And I had to rewind that part 20 times too. From "Steve Biko (Stir It Up)", Tribe kept the energy going with the next song, starting with some jazzy vibes to kick off the song "Award Tour" featuring Dave (Plug 2) of De La Soul breathing one of Hip-Hop's most memorable sing-songy choruses:

We on award tour with Muhammad, my man/ Going each and every place with the mic in their hand/ New York, NJ, N.C., VA (With Q-Tip saying "riiiiight—true" peppered throughout the chorus).

The drums on "Award Tour" are knocking with the guitar rocking out—running in the background and Phife and Tip's *(do-dat do-dat doo-doo-dat-dat-dat)* lyrics were top notch and too much for me to handle in a boujee downtown Chicago office space. After "Award Tour", the lovely voice of the program comes back—letting me know the meaning of the album by saying:

> *Seven times out of ten we listen to our music at night/ Thus spawned the title of this program/ The word, maraud, means to loot/ In this case, we maraud for ears...*

Right into a dope bass line loop running behind Phife lamenting:

> *Went to Carvel to get a milkshake/ This honey ripped me off for all my loot cakes/ The car oh yeah there's money in my jacket/ Somebody broke into my ride and cold macked it/ Yo Tip I tell you man the devil's tryin' it/ But I'm goin' to stay strong cause I ain't buyin' it*

Then the beat drops, and Phife continues to talk about all the problems he has to face as a young Black man moving around in New York and Georgia (that everybody knows he goes to often). "8 Million Stories" is based on everyday scenarios of the life of Phife that puts him in some tight positions that are weighing on him mentally. Some problems revolve around his little brother wanting a Barney doll from a toy store or problems around females either trying to stick him for something or asking him for things or him being stood up waiting to go to a Knicks game or taking a flight to Georgia and ending up somewhere completely different than his intended destination. Listening to "8 Million Stories", I can relate to what Phife is going through, and it lines up with another native of Queens, Nas, talking about his need for a dark cloud to follow someone else other than him in "The World is Yours" on the classic *Illmatic* album. "8 Million Stories" is easily one of my favorite Hip-Hop songs of all time. I just love the feel of this song, and even though I never want this song to end, I love how it ends with Phife giving shout outs and Q-Tip rhyming a hook or chorus that sounds more like a prayer. *Help me out God I really need you/ I'm having problems/ help me out now.*

The first half of *Midnight Marauders* takes the listener on journeys around stories and themes, and one of the themes is the problems surrounding the use of the N-word. On the song "Sucka N****", Q-Tip talks about how young people use the word (*Now the little shorties say it all of the time*) and how rappers use the word in their lyrics (*And a whole bunch of n***** throw the word in they rhyme*) and he even talks about his own personal frustrations around not being able to stop himself from using that word as well (*Yo I start to flinch, as I try not to say it/ But my lips is like the oowop as I start to spray it*) This song made me reflect on my own personal use of the N-word. I love the song "Sucka N****" because the tone of the song is not preachy, but it gets the message across in a subtle but strong way. After "Sucka N****"— I hear the sound of voices being slowed down as if Shaheed's hand is on the record slowing the sound down and then he begins to move the record back-n-forth to reveal the drums of *Midnight* with the aesthetic of people talking on the street in the background. On this song, Q-Tip describes the scene of the city and the life of urban youth and their movements, saying things like:

> *For the ghetto child it seem to be the right time/ See, kids be getting stuck with jewels and fly gimmicks/ Shorty see the action and then start to mimic Running to the corner, the dice game is blazing/ Looking at the loot, it seems so amazing*

After Tip describes the lay of the land, he zooms into the life of a particular *urban individual* who enters into a dice game. This rhyme continues to track the movements of the protagonist through the urban world. After telling the urban individual's story, Q-Tip decides to give us a glimpse into his personal *beats, rhymes and life* as a *nocturnal animal* engaging in the nighttime ritual of creating art and music. This song seems to be a continuation of *Low End Theory's* "Everything is Fair" song and it also reminds me of a continuation of the Sprite commercial that Tribe did back in the day where Q-Tip says:

> *When we had a thirst to dance/ we did it all night*
> *When we had a thirst to rhyme/ we broke out the mics*
> *When we had a thirst to dress/ we went and got fresh*
> *Image is nothing/ but thirst (pause)/ thirst is everything*

At the end of "Midnight," the midnight marauder program voice comes back with some more facts about life that we should be aware of:

> *Did you know that the rate of AIDS in the Black and Hispanic community is rising at an alarming rate? Education is proper means for slowing it down*

After this timely message from the program, we hear Shaheed gettin' busy on the turntable again, scratching a dope vocal sample of a rock singer along with Rakim's vocals as Q-Tip and Phife sing, "*we can get down.*" Phife and Q-Tip's rhymes are a mix of braggadocio and dropping jewels at the same time:

> *My rhymes styles be blending like a Ron G tape/ My man where ya going, you can't escape/ When the Tribe is in the house that means nobody is safe/ How can a reverend preach, when a rev can't define/ The music of our youth from 1979/ We rap 'bout what we see, meaning reality/ From people busting caps and like Mandela being free/ Not every MC be with the negativity/ We have a slew of rappers pushing positivity*

This song is the perfect way to end the first half of a well-put-together album and, as a bonus, we get to see just how nice Shaheed is on the 1s and 2s, cutting up Rakim's voice saying *Why waste time on the microphone*. And of course we hear the program voice again letting us know who the members of A Tribe Called Quest are:

A Tribe Called Quest consists of four members/
Phife Dawg, Ali Shaheed Muhammad, Q-Tip,
and Jarobi/ A, E, I, O, U and sometimes Y

Midnight Marauders is a well-crafted album from start to finish. The production on this album is stellar, and it has lasted the test of time. It's hard but soft. Warm but not so cold to where you become uninterested. The ear candy on this album is too much to handle. My day and life was made when this album was released. Thank you Phife (RIP), Ali Shaheed Muhammad, Q-Tip and Jarobi. A, E, I, O, U and sometimes Y.

CHAPTER SIXTEEN

Midnight Marauders Part 2
A Tribe Called Quest

Written by Donald "Profound" DeVold

As I sat down to write this reflection, I thought about how I wanted to start. Do I want to listen to the album first, or do I want to start writing from my memory? I decided to shut everything off and put on my studio headphones to re-take this *Midnight Marauders* journey.

In 1993, I was a year out of high school navigating my way through the healthcare workforce. I had a monthly subscription to the Source Magazine like most Hip-Hop heads back then. I would always be on the lookout for my favorite artists to drop. So, when promos started about the new A Tribe Called Quest album *Midnight Marauders*, all I could do was get excited. Especially after their last release *The Low-End Theory*. I wondered how they could ever do better than *Low-End*? Is that even possible? This was going to be the 3rd album from Tribe, and I absolutely loved the first two albums, but can Tribe get even better??

Heck, I didn't want to answer that. I just knew I would be at the record store to get my copy the day it dropped. I was the kid that liked a variety of Hip-Hop artists and groups, but A Tribe Called Quest was my absolute favorite with De La Soul running a very close 2nd. What was I doing the day this album was released? I was working at Evanston Hospital. I didn't have enough time to leave work for lunch to get my copy, so I had to wait until I got off that afternoon. I didn't have a car yet, so the Chicago Transit Authority (the El-trains) was always my studio where I listened to most of my music. I used to ride the trains back and forth from Central St. (Evanston, IL) all the way to 95th St. (Chicago's Southside) with my headphones on and a backpack full of Hip-Hop music. I was looking forward to taking a ride on the train with the new Tribe album.

If you're reading this, you've already absorbed the first half of *Midnight Marauders* as my brother, iomos marad, wrote Pt. 1 of this reflection. Mine starts at the halfway point through the album, and this song's chorus still gets debated even after Q-Tip explains what the chorus says, *"Relax ya self girl please settle down."* Yes, I'm talking about "Electric Relaxation" with the Ronnie Foster "Mystic Brew" sample. OH MY GOD!! (Wait, let me calm down, I haven't even gotten to the "Oh My God" song yet). The bass line and drums are in perfect sync alongside the main groove of the sample. Some would label this a Hip-Hop love song, but in my opinion, this wasn't a love song. It is more of a playful song about flirting when you are trying to get to know that girl you are interested in.

> *Honey, check it out, you got me mesmerized/*
> *With your black hair and your fat-as** thighs*
> *Street poetry is my everyday but yo, I gotta stop when you trot my way/*
> *If I was working at the club, you would not pay/*
> *Ayo my man Phife Diggy, he got something to say/*

One thing I always loved about Tribe was the way Q-Tip and Phife verbally tossed it back and forth so effortlessly. They were subtle, smooth but powerful all at the same time. The video for "Electric Relaxation" matches the vibe completely. The visuals start with them riding in a cab. You see flashes of New York imagery as Tribe makes their way to a restaurant for something to eat. Inside, the vibe is very familiar. You have guys sitting at tables, women sitting at tables, everyone seems to be enjoying the mood. You can tell Tribe is playing on the system inside the restaurant because everyone is nodding in unison.

The one thing I notice about the restaurant scene is everybody seems pleasant; they seem like they're all having the best time ever. The smiles on everyone's face show it, especially the women. Yeah, I guess I would call this "Hip-Hop's version of how to flirt." This song is placed perfectly in the mix of everything else. This is the apex of the album.

Cue elevator music. The image on the front cover says, *KEEP BOUNCING*.

The beat drops hard for "Clap Your Hands". Ali Shaheed scratches "*clap ya hands now*" ("Hand Clapping Song" – The Meters) while the kick drum hits deep and the snare has a pop or more like slap to it, but together the drums hit in that familiar ATCQ-style. While the previous track "Electric Relaxation" was a slightly laidback, light-hearted flirtatious song, "Clap Your Hands", on the other hand, is a more straightforward "We are better emcees than you" song. Phife rhymes in the 1st verse...

> *The worse thing in this world is a sucka emcee/*
> *Favorite rap group in the world is EPMD/*
> *Can't forget the De La, due to originality/*
> *And if I ever went solo my favorite emcee would be me/*

Ah, the braggadocious flare in your style is one of the original traits of an emcee. Phife usually lets you know that he is down for a battle at any time, and Q-Tip lets you know the same thing with his more subtle and swagged-out style. The song ends with the narrator reminding us once again to "*Keep Bouncing.*"

As the journey continues, we come to "Oh My God" and the drums are still hard, but the bass line is what sticks out to me in this song. Sampled from Lee Morgan's "Absolutions," the bass line and how it is used is phenomenal. I have always been amazed at the producers who can take a sample and make their own groove with it. This is one of those songs. Tip and Phife are in-sync once again with Busta Rhymes serving up that *RAWR RAWR like a dungeon dragon* for the chorus, "*OH MY GOD, YES, OH MY GOD.*" The chorus is perfect because that is exactly what I say whenever I get to this song.

"Keep it Rollin" is produced by and features a verse from the Large Professor (aka Extra-P). You would think adding a different producer to an already-established sound of ATCQ would affect the chemistry. On the contrary, it does the opposite. It adds to the collective of an already-classic album. Large Professor's emcee ability stands out while rhyming alongside ATCQ. To hear the song from the original sample (Roy Ayers – "Feel like Making Love") you quickly realize the genius of Large Professor on production.

The song to end this album, "God Lives Through", has a smooth jazzy sample that plays slightly in the background while the drums hit hard in ATCQ fashion. Again, you can hear Busta in the background of the chorus "OH MY GOD, OH MY GOD!" along with a horn sample that is featured just enough throughout the song.

My favorite part of this song is the chorus leading into the 2nd verse. You can hear Q-Tip singing...

> *La, la, la, la*
> *Doop, doo, do, do*
> *La, la, la, la*
> *Shooby-doop, do, do*
> *La, la, la, la*
> *We got the funk doody don sh**, clearly, it's the bomb sh**/*
> *So, recognize me kids memorize me*

The way Q-Tip slides right into the 2nd verse from the chorus is so smooth. After this song plays, I hit repeat again just to hear it one more time. Sitting here having just listened to this album yet again, all I can think is that *Midnight Marauders* ends just as exciting as it started. From the "Midnight Marauders Tour Guide" to "God Lives Through", this is a must-listen. Coming up on 30 years later from the release date of this album, it still feels and sounds like it belongs today, which is why it is still in my rotation of music. If you have never heard *Midnight Marauders*, do yourself a favor... LISTEN TO IT!

CHAPTER SEVENTEEN

Buhloone Mindstate
De La Soul
Written by MC Till

"Please, please, can we go to the record store?" I'm not sure if this is a direct quote, but it's probably close. The year was 1993. I was thirteen, and I needed *Buhloone Mindstate* in my life. Catch that? I didn't just want it. I needed it. If my current eleven-year-old tells me she "needs" something, I correct her. She doesn't need it. She wants it. Well, this was different. I needed that album! Hahaha. But it was true. I needed it. So at some point, my mom drove me to the record store, and we came home with what is currently my favorite album of all time. That might change. It could switch back to *The Low End Theory*. But today, it remains *Buhloone Mindstate*.

This is the album where it all comes together musically. The first two De La Soul albums were adventures. They were stories with skits, songs that were skits, and skits that were songs. Inside jokes and outside jokes were everywhere. Samples upon samples upon samples. They were experiences. One lives into those albums differently than other music projects. They were truly revolutionary. But they were full...perhaps too full for some. And perhaps too much for some. There was a lot happening on both of those albums. *Buhloone Mindstate* is different. It is more focused musically. There are samples but not as many. The skits are more like interludes, and not as silly. All the De La Soul elements are present. It's just that their presence created a very different experience.

That experience starts before it pops. Yeah, it might blow up, but it won't go pop. The listener hears this line repeat itself over and over again until it, well, pops. "*Mess up my mind, mess up my mind, mess up my mind with the eye patch.*" De La Soul wastes no time to display their lyrical posterity. On *3 Ft High & Rising*, Pos and Dave introduced the world to a very different way of rhyming. They continued that unorthodox delivery on *De La Soul is Dead*. But on *Buhloone Mindstate*, they perfect it. It does not sound like Rakim or Kool G Rap. It is not the foreshadowing of Nas or Snoop. Instead, it is the molding of a one-of-a-kind vocal presence. Especially with Pos, no one ever sounded like him before him, and no one has sounded quite like him still. His words contort and turn before finding the rhyme, but when they land, it is beautiful.

The messages run deep throughout the album. They are sometimes subtle like in "Patti Dooke" where they address cultural appropriation through metaphor and wit. Sometimes, the message on *Buhloone Mindstate* is masked behind sarcasm. "Ego Trippin" is a perfect example. De La Soul magnificently uses satire to reflect the absurdity of a shallow egocentric representation of Hip-Hop. "3 Days Later" manages to touch on the risk of casual sexual experiences and police brutality. Their way of shining light is not to turn on the flashlight and aim it directly at the listener. They spark a small match, barely bright enough to see it. But it grows with each listen. This is an album one can listen to a thousand times and still receive a lyric in a new refreshing way.

If it sounds like the album is too brainy, don't worry. The musicianship gives the listener plenty to enjoy. It is relaxing. It cuts through everything happening in 1993. Just one week after *Buhloone Mindstate* hit the shelf at your favorite record store, KRS-One, Souls of Mischief, and Spice 1 all released seminal projects. A few months later, Wu-Tang would emerge with their debut on the same day A Tribe Called Quest blessed us with

Midnight Marauders. That year also gave us classics from Black Moon, Digable Planets, and many more. Needless to say, it was an incredible year for Hip-Hop albums. And yet with all those classics proliferated with amazing music, this *Buhloone Mindstate* album is distinct. It's not Snoop's classic that sold a kajillion copies. It's not ONYX that made us all SLAM (*da du du, da du du, Let the boys be boys*). When you ask De La stans what their favorite De La album is, they don't normally mention this album. However, if you sit down and take the music in, you will find the perfect union of soul, jazz, and boom bap.

Prince Paul talked with Open Mike Eagle on his phenomenal program *What Had Happened Was* about the process of recording this album. On the first two albums, he was much more hands-on. By this third album, Pos, Dave, and Maseo are in the driver's seat while Prince Paul is giving directions in shotgun when necessary. One thing he mentioned that he did do was to bring in some legendary musicians to provide live instrumentation. The jazz and soul are both sampled *and* played in real time. Nowhere is this more evident than on "I Am I Be" which features Maceo Parker, Fred Wesley, and Pee Wee Ellis. The very next song is "In the Woods" and might be my favorite (although I say that about every song on here:). It features one of my favorite guest appearances ever. Shortie No Mass pops up to make the song even better. The horns on this song are breathtaking. They come in a few different ways and each change-up is perfect. The energy of the horns and the verses build synergy and climax around the 2:30 mark with some scratching sounds.

One last note on the music. Bass. There are two songs that feature a tactic that I love. The bass plays for a moment then abruptly stops either on a snare or downbeat. On "Eye Patch," the time between the bass playing is plenty. The bass only comes in every several measures. The absence of the bass lets the drums carry the load until the bass returns to give assistance. "Area" features a similar type of bass, but this time, it does the heavy lifting on almost every measure. However, it is taken out a few times, which allows the breakbeat to breathe. This in-and-out type of bass on both songs creates a really warm experience for the listener. It allows us to appreciate both bass and drums even more.

Buhloone Mindstate doesn't have the elaborate skits like De La Soul's two preceding albums. It doesn't have a smash single like "Me, Myself, and I." It is often overlooked during De La Soul's greatest album conversations. Still, I'm convinced that if any fan of music, specifically early 90s Hip-Hop, sits down and gives this album their undivided attention, they will find something amazing. They will find inviting lyrics that engage and re-engage with each listen. They will hear live instrumentation mixed with samples, drums, and bass that all work in tandem to produce beauty. I've enjoyed this album's beauty for nearly 30 years now, and I suspect I'll enjoy it another 30 more, God willing. When I bought the tape all those years ago, I needed it because *3 Feet High and Rising*, along with *De La Soul is Dead*, were my favorite albums. I knew this third De La album was going to be just as good. I was wrong. It was even better.

CHAPTER EIGHTEEN

Stakes is High for a 16-Year-Old Too
De La Soul

Written by MC Till

A few weeks after my 16th birthday, I met my girlfriend at the mall. She had a present for me. Not just any present though. What she placed in my hands would go on to be my favorite piece of art for years. She gave me *Stakes is High* by De La Soul. It was a Friday, and I remember going home that night, grabbing my Discman, sitting down at an old wooden table in our living room and pressing play. I think I listened to the entire album that night. I couldn't stop. It was one great song after another for seventeen songs: seventeen reasons to love this album. I won't list all seventeen here (just read the track listing), but I will celebrate a few and place them in the context of one young sixteen-year-old De La fan.

The album begins with people responding to the question, "Where were you when you first heard *Criminal Minded*?" Being that I was only 7 when that Boogie Down Productions album came out, I have no idea where I was. I hadn't even heard that album at that point. But being already so steeped in Hip-Hop, I knew the reference and could appreciate the cultural significance of the reference. So then these thumping drums come in with a ballooning bass line. The beat is simple, and it centers the rest of the album around a no-nonsense approach. Their first two albums were filled with skits. Their third album detracted from this approach a bit, but here on their fourth album, De La Soul replaces the lighthearted skits for just a few interludes, most of which are musical, not whimsical or silly. Even though the last question we hear on this album is, "Where were you when you heard *3 Feet High and Rising?*" this album is far from *3 Feet*. This is De La Soul taking the reins and giving us dope Hip-Hop music. Nothing less, nothing more.

Dave and Pos are once again brilliant on the mic. I love how Pos is able to meander words across the beat, allowing them to rhyme when necessary. Dave's a bit more straightforward, which provides great balance. Lyrically, I think this album is as good if not better than any other De La Soul release (minus *Buhloone Mindstate*). I especially enjoy the serious tone. It works really well over the production. This more serious tone also jived well with me and where I was at in my life. This was right around the time I got my driver's license. As I stated earlier, I had a girlfriend, a pretty steady one at that. I could still be really silly, but I was also discovering myself in some new ways. I was forming a new identity separate from youthful innocence.

Like the trio's approach to the production on this album, I was becoming more responsible for my life's decisions. The beats, with just a few exceptions, are all produced by De La Soul themselves. They all sound great too. From the intro to "Supa Emcees" to "Itzsoweezee (HOT)" to "Sunshine" to everything else in between, De La provides us a breakbeat-driven, subtle sample fest. It is beautiful. Nothing is glaring. Nothing is over-produced nor under-produced. Every sound on the album is perfectly placed, yet it doesn't sound polished. It has a rugged feel, and it also sounds smooth. The sound of the album can simultaneously provide an underground backpacker the opportunity to do the screw face ("The Bizness") while also winning over the ears of the casual Hip-Hop listener ("Stakes is High"). The production perfectly captured their crossroads and mine. Theirs was one of leaving Prince Paul's influence and venturing off into their own thing.

Mine was one of becoming my own person separate from my parents and close family.

Sometimes, this new territory can be scary. I wonder if it was like this for Posdnous, Dave, and Maseo. Prince Paul had essentially been the fourth member of De La Soul up to that point. He helped craft the first three albums which, as far as I'm concerned, are all classics. Then with *Stakes is High*, he had very little to nothing to do with it. After three darn near masterpieces of art, Plugs 1, 2, and 3 were on their own. It felt like they had something to prove, like they had a chip on their shoulder. I'm not sure I felt this same way. But I do remember wanting to impress others. I was getting more and more into music, and I wanted to make an impression. I wanted my musical reputation to precede me. So yeah, I guess in a way, I had something to prove too. I had something I wanted the world to know. I was an emcee and, if given the chance, I'd capture your attention with something dope.

De La Soul definitely gave us something dope with *Stakes is High*. After creating three classics while sharing the driver's seat with Prince Paul, the pressure was on. It was their moment of truth, and they definitely met the moment with excellence. They were at a turning point and made it look easy, much easier than my teenage existence. This album helped me with that awkward time by providing me hours of inspiration and comfort. To this day, if I need to be reminded that the world is not out to get me, I'll put this album on and forget about my troubles. I can't tell you where I was when I first heard *Criminal Minded*, but I can definitely tell you where I was when I first heard *Stakes is High*. I was in my living room, a blossoming 16-year-old finding my identity with the assistance of De La Soul.

CHAPTER NINETEEN

Beats, Rhymes & Life
A Tribe Called Quest

Written by Beau Brown

The heart has its reasons of which reason knows nothing." This oft-quoted line from 17th-century philosopher Blaise Pascal pretty much sums up how I feel about *Beats, Rhymes and Life*. The fourth album from A Tribe Called Quest was perhaps their most successful out of the gate. Yet, to many Tribe fans, it was considered subpar compared to the standard that had been set with their previous three albums. But then there's me...a kid who somehow found his way to the Native Tongues through the music video for Q-Tip's "Vivrant Thing." So, as I began my exploration into De La Soul, Black Sheep, the Jungle Brothers, and of course, ATCQ, my first stop was, you guessed it, *Beats, Rhymes and Life*.

In 1999, I had never heard of battle rap. So, hearing the first track, "Phony Rappers," was part of my enlightenment. Hearing rappers brag and boast, comparing their rhyme skills to some unnamed opponent, introduced me to the competitive aspects of Hip-Hop. As a result of this introduction, I spent the next 3 or 4 years typing "emcee battles" into my favorite search engine, being mesmerized by underground battlers like Supernatural and Eyedea. I found out pretty quickly that this was part of the very foundation of Hip-Hop, and Q-Tip and Phife were drawing on and re-interpreting a tradition that was integral to the Hip-Hop aesthetic.

The next few songs gave me the chance to get to know this new beatmaker who went by the name of Jay Dee. I wasn't really sure how Hip-Hop production worked at that point, but I knew there was something different and special about this guy. I had already fallen in love with Outkast a few years earlier, and the beats of Organized Noize were honestly the only comparison I could make to this new sound. These laid back, chill, simple beats were a nice counterpoint to the Cash Money/No Limit sound that was taking over radio at the time. Whether or not these beats were as great as some of Dilla's later work, they still changed my perception of how rhythm and melody can interact with a rapper's voice.

And then....and then...and then...there was "1nce Again!" Years later, I still find myself randomly picturing Tip and Phife on stage asking each other if they're on point. What a great way to start a song! And I've always been a sucker for a female-voiced hook, and Tammy Lucas's 'oooooh' and 'onanonanon' gave me all the good vibes I could handle. Once the beat shifted toward the verse, Phife just came out of the gate swinging. From *This is the year that I come and I just devastate...* to *by the end of the day, you'll be on my jock* to *you gots to do this from your heart, meaning your inner soul*, Malik had so many memorable lines in this song. To this day, "1nce Again" is easily in my Top 5 songs of all time.

This album was also my introduction to the "social" element of Hip-Hop. I'm quite certain that they didn't set out to make a "social" song with "Stressed Out," but that was the effect it had on me. My eyes were opened by the narration of a high-stress situation told through the lens of a man hoping to rise above poverty by shooting dice, while trying to avoid violence and get some relief from the pressure of, among other things, having a baby on the way. The storytelling skill of Consequence and Q-Tip put me right there in that situation, placing me on a lifelong path to understand and challenge the societal injustices that cause the type of stress narrated in this song. Hearing Faith Evans sing, "we're gonna make it" as the album fades away is simply beautiful.

There aren't many records out there that I can truly say changed my life, but *Beats, Rhymes and Life* is on that level. Maybe they weren't "innovating" as much anymore, but they certainly innovated my listening habits from that point on. So, even if my increasingly discerning ear for Hip-Hop tells me this is not ATCQ's best album, my heart tells me it doesn't matter. Thank you, heart.

CHAPTER TWENTY

Sept 29, 1998: A Great Day for Natives: The Love Movement, the Foundation, & the Black Star
A Tribe Called Quest - Brand Nubian - Black Star

Written by MC Till

I vividly remember the day. I had been preparing for weeks. Spotify didn't exist then. Neither did YouTube or Bandcamp. If I wanted to listen to an album over and over again, I had to buy it. That's exactly what I had in mind on Tuesday, September 29, 1998. The only problem was that I needed to buy 3 new albums that day. *The Love Movement* by A Tribe Called Quest, *Mos Def & Talib Kweli are Black Star*, and *Foundation* by Brand Nubian. So for a few weeks leading up to this historic release day, I was saving my money. I didn't have a job at the time, but I needed the money. Now I've never told anyone this before, but what I would do is pocket some or all of my lunch money for a few weeks so that I could buy new CDs. My mom would give me $3 each day for lunch. I would maybe buy a salad for $1 and save the other $2. Sorry mom. At least I was eating healthy! When I had enough saved up, I would go get the CD I wanted. But I had a problem on 9/29/1998. I only had enough for 2 of the 3 CDs I wanted.

I knew Brand Nubian well. I had all their previous CDs or tapes already. Same with Tribe. Logically, I had to get those two CDs, and I did. I didn't want to do anything else that day but listen to them. I remember it was homecoming week my senior year of high school and my classmates wanted me to come out and help build the senior float. Sorry guys. I had something important to do... listen to new Hip-Hop. That's exactly what I did that night. I sat down and listened to both albums from beginning to end. Needless to say, it was an incredible night.

Some are not big fans of *The Love Movement* by A Tribe Called Quest. I don't know why. This album features thick bass lines, booming kick drums, crisp snares, excellently placed high hats and shakers and sampling/instrumentation that meanders around the drums to perfection. While all that is taking place, Phife Dawg and Q-Tip display as much if not more style on this album than any of their previous releases. They are gliding across beats winking at listeners, pointing at bystanders, and just enjoying the music. I know that might feel a bit ironic since we know that they were about to break up, and in real life, apparently they were not enjoying one another! Or at least they were not getting along well enough to keep going.

But let's not allow historical hindsight to hinder the enjoyment. Take "Find A Way." That song is darn near Hip-Hop perfection. Listen to how Q-Tip introduces verse two, *Now why you want to go and do that love huh?* The beat fades out, an echo appears, as does a sample, then when the beat drops again, it feels divine. Nothing profound lyrically, but when taken with the overall sound, Phife and Tip become one with the music.

Being that Tribe is my second favorite group of all time, following closely behind De La Soul, I naturally listened to *The Love Movement* first. After that, it was all about the return of Brand Nubian! I was probably looking forward to that album even more than Tribe's. Grand Puba hadn't reunited with Sadat X and Lord Jamar for several years, and now they were back on one album together. But was it going to be any good? YES!

Foundation features 20 tracks, and only a few are interludes. With the exception of two beats, I like every song on that album. So that's like an entire hour of dope! The first song on the album, "The Return", is produced by DJ Premier, and it sounds like it with those drums, chopped sample, and scratched hook. It is pure Brand Nubian bliss. So right off the bat, they come out swinging, and I recall being in my bedroom as a kid with a huge smile on my face. Then, "Shinin' Star" comes in, and it delivers too. It has a very upbeat, positive feel. "The Beat Change" comes next and it has a funky, throwback feel. I was loving this album already, but then their lead single "Don't Let it Go to Your Head" plays next, and I remember thinking how much I was going to love this album after those four songs. The album continues to be dope throughout. Well, except for the production on "Let's Dance" and "Too Late." I was not feeling those beats. Still don't get into them. But hey, maybe you do!

Okay, *Foundation* was dope. *The Love Movement* was dope. I was ready to go to bed. But wait, what about *Black Star*? Well, like I said before, it was a different time back then. Sadly, I didn't hear that album until several months later. But it was certainly worth the wait! That opening sequence of the "Intro", "Astronomy (8th Light)", "Definition", and "Re:Definition", is one of the best, most Hip-Hop beginnings of an album ever. It sets up the listener so well. The intro informs us that Mos Def and Talib Kweli are more than entertainers. They are historians on the mic. "Astronomy" warms us up with a bunch of questions. It gets us thinking. It engages us. The beat, stirred up by the Beatminerz, is the perfect backdrop for Mos and Kweli to trade intellectual verses over. Now that we are all warmed up and ready to go on this ride, they give us "Definition" where they summon the spirits of Scott La Rock and Boogie Down Productions. Mos and Kweli are present on the mic in a way that doesn't suggest authority but claims it and then exudes it. They are in control. We are invited to the party, but they are definitely the hosts, the emcees. We finish this introductory sequence with a clever flip of "Definition" for "Re:Definition." From there, we get all kinds of interesting songs, including a remake of Slick Rick's "Children's Story", an ode to brown skin women ("Brown Skin Lady"), a dedication to B-boys ("B Boys will Be Boys"), a top-tier posse cut in "Twice Inna Lifetime", and a contender for greatest Hip-Hop song ever with "Respiration." Like the two albums I listened to on that lovely day in September, *Black Star* is an album of excellence.

There it is. One of the greatest days in Hip-Hop gave us three incredible albums that Native Tongues fans could enjoy and celebrate. I sure did. If you were not a fan of any one of these albums, I invite you to revisit that album or revisit all three. Give them a listen all the way through. Let them sit in your soul. Give them license to lead you and see where they take you this time around. I am so thankful I was able to do that all those years ago. I loved all three albums then and I still do today. Thank you, September 29, 1998.

CHAPTER TWENTY-ONE

The Grind Date
De La Soul

Written by Dayne Hall

When you are given a 30+ year career in an ever-changing industry, you are the epitome of a champion. Musically, you probably have so much content to filter through. It is easy to assume that every consumer of Hip-Hop music would absolutely love the heralded classics. I'm reminded of ATCQ with *The Low End Theory*. How about The Roots with *Illadelph Halflife*? Of course, we can't forget an album like *Stakes is High*, but what if I told you none of these albums were my favorite from each group? You'd probably want to revoke my Hip-Hop card, right? Haha. Technically, I'm still on the fence about some of these albums not being my favorite, if we are keeping records. Hopefully, that salvages some of the damage. Lol. The larger point I'm making here is that with an extensive catalog, there will likely be different starting points of when you, the listener, started tuning into said artist.

I was having a short discussion recently, and mid-conversation, a term closely linked to Hip-Hop culture was uttered, "Once again it's on." My friend quickly pointed out how the very mention of that saying, more like a Hip-Hop colloquialism, will forever remind him of a certain De La Soul song. Like a true Hip-Hop head, I took that as a challenge to guess the song.... boom! It was then and there I started nodding my head, trying to remember the lyrics word for word as I had the beat cued in my mind.

> *I'm a take it at the horns till the pinky toe torn /*
> *And show you why we here this long /*
> *Cause when it comes to puttin' in work /*
> *Once again it's on*

Fast forward to now, which is the perfect segue to speak about how that song, which also serves as the album title, has affected me. Ladies and gents, I'm talking about *The Grind Date* by De La Soul.

As mentioned earlier, it is easy to mention the expected classics in Hip-Hop conversations. I'd be lying if I said I have never indulged in knowing more about an album or artist than I really did to preserve my "Hip-Hopness" if you will. The things we do for pride. Back in the day, when *The Source* was "The Source," I relied heavily on general consensus to guide my musical taste. As times have evolved, I quickly realized that, like many things that once held significance, with time they fade. I stopped collecting *The Source* like I once did. My Hip-Hop posters got replaced with fresh white paint, and a notebook app on my cell phone became my new pen and pad. I was at a different place in my life. I wasn't consuming as much new music as I once did. I started relating to Andre 3000 in a sense, as I started losing inspiration to write as well. In retrospect, what I really needed was simply to go through real-life experiences.

In my quest for deeper meaning, I found myself going back to older albums. I needed something sonically that could serve as the soundtrack to my life. A little Nas here, some Brand Nubian there and so on and so forth. Once I familiarized myself with most of the certified classics, I found myself yearning for something "new." I wasn't one to buy many CDs at this point, but *The Grind Date* was one album I had to have. I didn't know what to expect with this album. Oddly enough, I still remember *The Source* giving *The*

Grind Date 3 ½ mics. I thought I had bought a blank copy, to be honest. I pressed play on my Sony system, and I heard nothing for the first few seconds.... ahhhh! "There it is," I said to myself as I started faintly hearing Maseo's voice gradually rise through the speakers. "We are the present, we are the future, we are your past," he said, in an almost indoctrinating tone. Well, I guess it worked because I was hooked!

I quickly realized that this album was different from De La's prior releases. For one, at 13 tracks, this was a much shorter album than what I had grown accustomed to from them. They also seemingly ditched a lot of their abstract tendencies. No skits too. Coming off of the *AOI* series, I could visibly see by *The Grind Date*'s album cover that this release was a more down-to-earth (literally), blue-collared offering. No space suits this time around.

At first listen, I knew I loved this album. It was so soulful, easily digestible, sonically seamless, relatable, and sprinkled with real-life quotables.

> *They say the meek shall inherit the earth but don't forget the poor are the ones who inherit the debt.*

I absolutely loved it! I couldn't pick a favorite. Some days, it was the silky smooth "It's Like That" featuring Carl Thomas. He crushed the hook, by the way, and finessed it at the end. "It's De La....and I got the soul." Some days, it was the crunchy and unorthodox MF DOOM-assisted "Rock Co.Kane Flow." There were so many moments to choose from. If you ask me today, I'd say it's the easy-going but crisp, intentful lyricism and delivery on "Days of Our Lives." This is a sign of a great album, people. I sort of feel guilty leaving some songs off, as they are all worthy of honorable mention.

This was exactly what I needed at the exact time I received it. This was the album that would loosely serve as the soundtrack to my personal life. This album had the perfect amount of reality (see the hook on "Church"), optimism, and maturity that I was yearning for. This was the first time I saw De La Soul not in character. I always saw them as quirky comic book characters for some reason. I think they literally were in a cartoon recently. Yes, *Teen Titans GO!* They were the quirky artists that could yell all over a hook ("Ego Trippin 2"), have a full-fledged food fight in a cafeteria ("Itzsoweezee"), and make a song about pulling a pistol on Santa Claus. Haha. So it was rather refreshing to see one of my favorite groups become more relatable to me.

As I look at *The Grind Date* CD, which is still in pristine condition, the cover brings back so many memories. If I had to recommend any De La Soul album to a casual Hip-Hop fan to start with, this album would be the first I'd mention. It is perfectly balanced. Sonically, it plays very well. The song sequencing is near-perfect. The features are not forced. They are tastefully executed. The overall mood is optimistic, but there is just the right amount of reality-based trials and tribulations to create a "we shall prevail" aura. The soulful samples make for a seamless overall aesthetic. I guess you can tell, I really love this album.

It's amazing how things come around full circle. I touched on heralded classics to open up this thesis, and as I complete my final words...I'm realizing *The Grind Date* may be that heralded classic I spoke of. I believe that much in this album. I truly believe that this is one of De La's most important releases. If there's one takeaway this album has taught me, it's that timing is everything. And when it comes to my love for Hip-Hop, thanks to this album...."once again, it's on."

CHAPTER TWENTY-TWO

A Tale of Two Returns

Written by MC Till

Way back in 2016, it had been 12 years since De La Soul released a group album and 18 years since A Tribe Called Quest released an album. This drought from both groups definitely left a ridiculous amount of fans thirsting for some new Native Tongue tunes. I know I was hungry for more. A Tribe Called Quest is my second favorite group of all time right behind De La Soul. So when I heard that De La Soul had a Kickstarter going to record and release a new album, and then I heard Tribe had a final album in the works with Phife, I was ecstatic. I couldn't wait. I gave money to the Kickstarter to ensure I would get an early copy of the De La album and I called Everybody's Records (local record store in Cincinnati, OH) and reserved my A Tribe Called Quest album weeks before its arrival. (Thanks, Woody).

Then, they arrived. De La Soul's *...and the Anonymous Nobody* came first. I ripped off the wrapper of the CD and popped it in immediately. What followed was over an hour of slow-moving, funky, therapeutic, eclectic, Hip-Hop. Honestly, upon first listen, there were a few standout songs that captured me instantly like "Property of Spitkicker.com" featuring Roc Marciano and "Whoodeeni" featuring 2 Chainz. I found these songs, along with a few others, entertaining as soon as I heard them. Other songs, however, took some time for me to fully enjoy. Two such songs finish the album. "Here in After" and "Exodus" don't sound anything like De La Soul's earlier work. Pos and Dave barely rap on them trading in bars for singing. These songs are also less traditional Hip-Hop in sound and more alternative rock. After Dave sings and raps a little, "Here in After" turns into a 3-minute Damon Albarn song. Is there anything wrong with that? No. Is it what I was expecting from De La Soul? No. These two songs illustrate how I grew to appreciate this album. I found many songs, at first listen, either just okay or simply different. But upon the third and fourth and 87th listens, I started to really enjoy every song on the album.

What I appreciate most about this album is how laidback it is. Even the more upbeat songs like the Snoop-assisted "Pain" have a very chill feel to it. One of the most chill songs is co-produced by Pete Rock and features Estelle's beautiful voice along with lush strings. "Memory of... (US)" is simply beautiful even if it took a few spins to finally get into it. Even my least favorite song on the album, "Greyhounds", featuring Usher has a very calm, relaxing vibe to it accompanied by great writing. That's what this album is: brilliant writing coupled with a feeling of calm sprinkled with moments of traditional boom bap and rock 'n' roll. It sounded different from all their other albums, but I was pleased and having listened to it for about a month straight, I was ready for this new Tribe album.

About 2 months later, it came with the longest album title in Hip-Hop history, *We got it from Here... Thank You 4 Your Service.* Phife apparently came up with the name and no one is 100% sure what he was thinking. But everyone is 100% thankful that he was a real part of this album. This wasn't a posthumous situation where they were lifting old Phife verses. He was a part of making this album. It gets better. Not only was Phife there helping craft this album, but Jarobi was too! He is featured on several tracks and sounds impeccable. Jarobi, Phife, and Q-Tip sound right back at home. Busta Rhymes and Consequence also show up on several songs to add more family comfort.

Okay, we know who the main players are. How is the music? Pretty dope. Sort of like the De La Soul album, some songs really stuck out to me instantly while others took a few listens to get into. Whereas De La Soul experimented more outside of Hip-Hop with more rock influence, Q-Tip and Tribe seemed to experiment within the solid walls of Hip-Hop. Sometimes it really worked for me like the vocal effects present on "We the People..." Sometimes, it felt like overkill, like on the drum programming toward the middle of "Lost Somebody" or the extra echoes and such overpowering Jarobi's verse on the opener, "The Space Program." Overall, it was just so wonderful to hear A Tribe Called Quest back together again. It was also super sad since Phife passed away in the midst of the crew getting back together.

I've seen many people criticize both albums. Some think the De La album is a snooze fest. Others think Tribe is a scattered mess. Music hits us all differently which is really beautiful. It is the same exact notes being played, the same lyrics rapped, but each set of ears they fall on are the entry into a one-of-a-kind soul. Each soul will receive the music differently. Regardless of how they land in your soul, one must appreciate the significance of these two albums. When Tribe and De La started out, they both released their first, second, third, and fourth albums in the same year ('91, '93, '96). With Phife's passing, they had one more shot and they did it. They released these albums in the same year just months apart. That's pretty cool.

De La Soul and A Tribe Called Quest are two of the greatest Hip-Hop groups of all time. They pioneered new trends in music. They sold millions of albums. They toured the world. They accumulated a shared fan base that rejoiced like I did just hearing the news they had new music coming out. Their place in Hip-Hop has been solidified many times over, and neither group is finished. The rumor is that De La Soul has a lot more music in the works. I'm confident Q-Tip is working on something right now. Jarobi, too. And Ali Shaheed Muhammad (who was absent for the recording of their final album for unknown reasons) together with Adrian Younge is on volume 9 of their dope *Jazz is Dead* series. They've been around for more than three decades and are still giving us more to appreciate.

CHAPTER TWENTY-THREE

Here Goes Nothing
Shortie No Mass

Written by MC Till

Guess who's back? Shortie No Mass! Yes, the dope emcee who emerged on *Buhloone Mindstate* and in some ways stole the show when she appeared. She was phenomenal. Her voice, her thoughts on the mic, her presence brought so much value to an already masterful performance from De La Soul. I was just minding my business on Thursday afternoon, December 16, 2021, when I saw someone on Facebook post about a new Shortie No Mass album! What?!! Actually, to be honest with you, I was upset before I heard the news. My kids had been stressing me out with their frustrating behavior. I was still in my feelings about that when I heard about this new album. Well, those sad, frustrated feelings left my soul with the quickness. How could I be upset when I had a new Shortie No Mass album to experience?

Let's go. The very first thing I heard on the album was Shortie rapping on that classic De La Soul song "In the Woods." Then Phife Dawg comes on asking Terressa (her name at birth) for some new music. A modern boom bap beat comes in glaring with a Native Tongues vibe. Moments later, Shortie No mass spits a verse and just two bars in, she pays homage to Phife Dawg. Oh, and she sounds as fresh today as she did all those years ago on *Buhloone Mindstate*. This is going to be good. One verse and done. On to the next.

On "Who's Shortie", she asks and answers that question with confidence. She lets us know she came up with the Native Tongues and is as fresh as anyone around. So who is she? She responds with "She's legit one of the best who ever did it." So has she lost a step? No, and she gives no excuses. Instead, she owns her craft, "I can do it when I want and that's the best f'ing part." She is in control.

As confident and dope as she sounds, Shortie No Mass is still human. "Identity Crisis" reveals some inner wrestling as she questions, *Which way to go, mainstream or straight Hip-Hop? This f'ing struggle never stops.* This line of questioning always makes me nervous. I always want my favorite emcees to go straight Hip-Hop and not worry about commercial viability. Thankfully, we get nothing but Hip-Hop throughout *Here Goes Nothing*. The very next song after "Identity Crisis" is the title track, where we hear Shortie No Mass let go by saying, *F it, here goes nothing.*

It is almost as if she knows people are going to be harsh, judging her every word, sound, look, etc. She is probably correct. There are always people who can't just let other people be. They have their expectations and try to keep people trapped inside them. I'm sure there are some who only remember Shortie No Mass from *Buhloone Mindstate* and will not be able to separate her from that classic album. I would suspect she knows that people will hold her up against that album. And how does she respond? "F' it, here goes nothing." I love the confident, carefree attitude, and I'm glad she has it so that we now get this new music!

There are a few things I especially love about this album. First and foremost, her voice is one of my favorites. Her voice and delivery work so well together. I also love the consistency from song to song. This project, however short, flows really well. Now, what I don't love is the project's brevity. It contains 9 songs with 3 of those songs clocking in right around a minute. I wish this album was longer. However, I can't appreciate what isn't yet created. I can appreciate what is though. And what is featured on this short project is 9 dope Hip-Hop tracks. We can only hope that this return project is just the beginning.

CHAPTER TWENTY-FOUR

Forever
Phife Dawg
Written by MC Till

Sometimes, I like to write about an album as I'm listening to it for the first time. Since I've been anticipating this one for years, I thought I'd do just that. This is not a well-thought-out review after having listened to the album over and over again. These are my thoughts in real time while I'm listening to the album. The only thing I do after I write a piece like this is go back and fix some grammar. So it is raw and immediate. Here we go.

"Cheryl's Big Son" featuring V.Rich
Quick intro with V.Rich singing just a bit over some strings and piano. Then, what appears to be a young Phife shows up talking with his mom's encouragement to speak up.

"Only a Coward"
Nice to hear from Phife again. He sounds comfortable over this soulful head-nodding beat from 9th Wonder. I like this. Great way to open the album.

"Fallback" featuring Rapsody and Renée Neufville
This is a lovely laidback groove filled with what appears to be bars about his family. Rapsody adds a nice feel to the mix. Feels like a summertime, nostalgic groove to me.

"Nutshell Pt. 2" featuring Busta Rhymes and Redman

Having already heard this, I am no less impressed by it. I love this joint. Love Phife's energy here as well as his guests. Each emcee builds on the kinetic synergy. And this beat from Dilla is beautiful. This sounds like something from *Love Movement,* but rougher, like a "Settin' It Up pt. 2" type of joint.

"Sorry" featuring V.Rich

Ohhhh, this beat comes in lovely. As soon as I heard that bass line, I thought, Nottz. I knew he had a few beats on here and, sure enough, he did this beat. Phife's verses remind me how much I love how he doubles up some bars, giving such texture to his recordings. It also sounds like he punches in at times. That's not a knock on him but a compliment, because he makes it artistically dope. I love his apologetic tone on this song too. Dope to hear his humility and honesty.

"Dear Dilla Reprise" featuring Q-Tip

This is a reprise of a joint he did over a Slum Village beat that originally featured Q-Tip, "Hold Tight." Because I love that original "Hold Tight" beat so much, this song will take some time for me to get used to. Anytime someone does a tribute to Dilla, I'm happy though. Q-Tip provides some nice crooning on the hook. I like it.

"Wow Factor" featuring Maseo

Not sure if I'm feeling this beat or not. There are elements that are dope. It has what sounds like a nice string sample and some vocal hits. It has potential. But I think the drums, especially the snares, don't hit as loud as I would like. Love how Phife is just rapping about things that he thinks are dope. That's cool. Not a bad joint. An okay joint. It features Maseo too, which is cool, but all he says is "Wow," which is fine but would have loved to hear him in a more prominent role. Always enjoy hearing the third Plug on the mic.

"Residual Curiosities" featuring Lyric Jones

Love that Lyric Jones is on this song. The beat has a very 1-2 punch to it demanding that my head nods. Similar to "Wow," though I feel like the drums could have been stronger. Might be a preference thing as I'm pretty picky when it comes to drums. But regardless, this is a pretty dope jam.

"God Send" featuring Dwele

Oh snap, I just noticed this song has production credit by G-Koop. He has done some pretty dope stuff in his career. I like the beat much better when the verse first starts. I'm not sure I'm feeling this beat overall though. It kind of sounds trapped in between crossover appeal and boom bap. It also features some synthesizer sounds, especially in the hook, and I've never been a fan of that sound. We'll see if it grows on me. It is definitely not bad, and I could see people really loving this joint. Again, I think it is a matter of personal preference. I do really enjoy what Phife is talking about though. He gives props to his family, friends, and wife who showed up during tough times. He finds a way to remain triumphant and positive even when things are not looking good. That's a dope message.

"Round Irving High School" featuring Cheryl Boyce-Taylor and Angela Winbush

Not sure if this is going to be a song with Phife on it or not. It features who I think is Ms. Cheryl reciting some poetic words over lush instrumentation. No drums, just heavenly-sounding piano, strings, and things. Now the poetic reciting turns to singing, an ode to Phife singing *I'll see you on the other side.* Back to poetic words. This isn't really a Phife song. Okay, it is not at all. But it's cool, and I appreciate it. Oh shoot, I'm just now realizing that is

Phife's mom. Okay, yeah, dope. I'm thankful they put this on the album.

"French Kiss Trois" featuring Redman and Illa J

I've heard this song many times before. There are some things I dig about this song, like the horns. Those horns are beautiful. But overall, I guess it is one of those songs where I don't really care for the lyrics. Phife does sound energetic, which is cool. Not bad but not a standout either, to me at least.

"2 Live Forever" featuring Pos and Little Brother

Oh yes! My favorite emcee of all time opens up this song but only spits a few bars before passing it off to Phonte of Little Brother. Maybe he'll be back. But this song is dope so far. I like the beat. I love hearing Pos and Little Brother. I like the sparse singing too. Okay, here comes Pos again. YES! That dude sounds so dope every time. The only downside to this song is I don't hear Phife except for at the end where we hear him talking, not rapping. Nice to hear him just talk though. Man, wish he was still here in the flesh.

"Forever"

Love the beat! Nottz is such an underrated, underappreciated producer. His way with bass lines has always been impressive. They are so thick and crackly, reminiscent of mid-90s Erick Sermon, but they have an original feel to them too. I like this song. Phife has a playful talk-rap style here, and I love it. He is just reminiscing, and I'm eating it up. Wish he could record more music forever!

Overall, I can't wait to listen to this album again and again to further appreciate one of my favorites, Phife Dawg. Rest in Power.

Part Three
Essays

CHAPTER TWENTY-FIVE

The Native Tongues Name

Written by iomos marad

Sometime in 1988 or the early 90s:

After getting back from Boston late last night, Q-Tip is thinking about making time and creating space in his busy schedule to hit a record store or two—knowing that he has a lot on his plate for that day. As he was envisioning himself in the record store buying the records he wanted to buy, he almost forgot that he had to connect with Bob, Ali, and Phife to listen to some mixes of new songs for the upcoming album. Then maybe after that, he can connect with Jarobi or Extra P to hit up some record stores. He continues to reorder his schedule in his head to ensure that he will end up at a record store at some point of the day.

As Tip walks into the record store laughing and joking with Jarobi, he walks straight to the Jazz section first. Q-Tip spends the majority of his time in this section thumbing through jazz greats like *Ahmad Jamal, Art Blakey, Charles Mingus, Freddie Hubbard, Gary Bartz, Lonnie Smith, Ron Carter,* and others. He strategically moves through the record store like a master digger—from Jazz to Reggae/Roots from Reggae/Roots to Rock and from Rock to Soul. Tip begins walking toward the cashout and stacks too many records to count on the counter. And as the cashier begins punching the prices on the cash register, Q-Tip decides to circle back to the Soul section, as if he is being summoned by the ancestors of soul to take one more look to see what he might find.

As Tip thumbs through the vinyl legacies of Soul greats, one particular album catches his eye. In bold Star Wars-like lettering reads *RCA THE NEW BIRTH*. Under the vibrant and bold lettering reads *Coming Together*. And right underneath the title leaping off the cover is a photo of a group of beautiful Black people with smiles on their faces. A photo capturing a moment of community, solidarity, and Black love. Q-Tip taps Jarobi—who followed him to the Soul section to dig again too—and says, "Yo, check this sh— out! I can't wait to get back to the flat to hear what's on this!"

Sometime around mid to late 1971 or early 1972

(The) New Birth—a funk and R&B group conceived in Detroit but now based in Louisville, Kentucky—are super excited about a song they just recorded entitled "African Cry" for their upcoming third album *Coming Together*, set to be released sometime in March '72, produced by the mentor of the group, Harvey Fuqua. Even though Fuqua is exhausted by all the challenges of putting this album together, he is still excited about the work and how well he and the other musicians and singers were able to work so well together during the making of the new project despite the challenges they faced.

As Fuqua is listening to the recording of "African Cry" with the engineer, he begins to reflect back to 1963-64 and the journey of how a collective of musicians and vocalists decided to come together based on an idea from his assistant, Vernon Bullock, who had been thinking about creating an ensemble of groups to become a touring company. This caught the interest of Fuqua and his brother in music, Tony Churchill, who began to recruit singers who they thought would be a great fit into this touring ensemble. The foundation of the ensemble would be an instrumental group called *The New Liters*, who helped to create a hit song with Chicago artist, Alvin Cash, called "Twine Time" in 1964—

moonlighting under the name *The Crawlers*. Before the formation of *New Birth,* the New Liters had a few hit songs. The New Liters band featured musicians like Churchill on tenor sax and vibes, Charlie Hearndon and later Carl McDaniel on guitar, James Baker on Keys, Robin Russell on drums (famous for his *Drum Beats* album), Robert "Lurch" Jackson on trumpet, Austin Lander on baritone sax, and LeRoy Taylor on bass.

The vocalists for this new ensemble revolved in and out, consisting of artists like Johnny Graham, who would eventually become a member of Earth, Wind & Fire, and Jerry Bell on lead and background vocals. There was a group called *The Now Sound* that Fuqua and Churchill discovered, featuring singers Bobby Downs, Ron Coleman, Gary Young, and George "Slim" House. Fuqua, Churchill, and Bullock also ran across a female vocal group called the *Mint Julep*, featuring Londee Loren, Tanita Gines, Janice Carter and Pam Swent. Even before the discovery of these singers, Alan Frye was originally brought in to sing with the New Liters. Later on, Bullock found another group out of Detroit by the name of *Love, Peace & Happiness*, featuring former Marvelettes singer Ann Bogen and brothers Leslie and Melvin Wilson. But in 1970, the New Liters, along with Londee Loren, Tanita Gaines, Janice Carter, Pam Swent, and Alan Frye reemerged on the scene under the name New Birth and released two albums on RCA. The first was a self-titled album, and the second album, *Ain't No Big Thing, But It's Growing*, made a little noise with a small hit record.

Later that year in '71, Bullock came across former Marvelettes singer Ann Bogen, Leslie and Melvin Wilson and thought they had the spark that was missing with the original members of New Birth: Londee Loren, Bobby Downs, and Alan Frye. In 1972, the New Birth ensemble was reorganized and re-energized by the new editions of vocalists and began working on the third album, entitled *Coming Together*.

After hearing the song "Indian Reservation" by Paul Revere & The Raiders Fuqua and the team decided to make an Afrocentric version of *Indian Reservation* to talk about the experiences of Black Africans being murdered, kidnapped, and stolen from Africa, similar to the experience of Indigenous people of North America who are the original owners of this land that we occupy today.

Somewhere in St. Albans Queens, Sometime in 1988, 1989, or the early 90s:

As Q-Tip settles in for the night looking through the albums he purchased early that day, he listens to a few records, vibing out with Jarobi. But it was while he was listening to a Charles Mingus album that Q-Tip noticed the picture of the New Birth album sticking out between a few other jazz records. He instantly remembers how he felt connected to the album at the record store based on the cover. He stops the turntable playing the Mingus album and puts it back into the jacket while grabbing the New Birth *Coming Together* album and places it on the turntable. "Two Kinds of People (I Am)" comes through the speakers first and Tip instantly looks at Jarobi to say without saying, "what is this!" "Oh Baby, I Love The Way*"* runs next with the bass line driving the sound in the back with the rhythmic tambourine keeping pace with Robin Russell on the drums. "Yesterday I Heard the Rain" was up next, with the thick soulful groove pushing the song with a crazy bass line and smooth melodic guitar riffs to bring that 70s vibe all the way through. The first three songs kind of put Q-Tip and Jarobi in a chill and relaxed mood listening to the aforementioned songs, but it wasn't until the horns at the beginning of "African Cry" took ahold of Tip and Jarobi and moved them both to jump up saying, "Yo! Are you hearing this! What is this!!! Yoooooo this is crazy! Word-Word-Word!"

As Q-Tip and Jarobi began to settle down, Tip really began to listen to the lyrics of the song, and his eyes instantly lit up like

Times Square or Shea Stadium as he began to reflect about a conversation he had with Afrika of the Jungle Brothers a couple of days ago about some brothers from Long Island whom Afrika met in Boston that Q-Tip had to meet. Afrika told Q-Tip, "Yo, I swear they are just like us." Q-Tip remembers getting to Boston and meeting these brothers who ended up being De La Soul.

After listening to the lyrics of "African Cry" the first time, Q-Tip knew the song was about the transatlantic slave trade where Black African people were stolen and kidnapped from their homeland and cut off from their history, culture, and language.

> *Took our whole Black African tribe*
> *Whipped our back and enslaved our minds*
> *Took away our shield and spear*
> *Shipped and shackled, chained and feared*

But after listening to the lyrics of "African Cry" countless times after the first time, the line that continued to stick with Q-Tip was:

> *Took away our Native Tongue*
> *Taught their English to our young*

Thinking about the conversation he had with Afrika and meeting De La Soul in Boston, Q-Tip started *ruminating* about how Hip-Hop culture has been a way for Black people to reclaim what has been taken away from them. Through slavery and the art of emceeing as a symbolic expression of speaking in a Native Tongue, Black people created a language that's spoken by people that's indigenous to that land. Likewise, all of us within Hip-Hop culture are speaking the same tongue, the same language. Q-Tip continued to think about how Hip-Hop is about being original individuals but how it's important to move within a community. Q-Tip brought this idea to Afrika, then they brought it to Posdnous of De La Soul, and the rest is history. A Hip-Hop legacy that can never be forgotten. Native Tongues is not only a dope name for a crew, but it is the philosophy of creating or reclaiming culture and the power of moving as a collective versus moving independently. This is why we (Boom Bap Chat/Everybody's Hip-Hop Label) are taking the time to celebrate the legendary Native Tongues movement for what they mean to us and for Hip-Hop culture overall.

CHAPTER TWENTY-SIX

3 Feet to 3 Decades: A Journey into Hip-Hop

Written by MC Till

I remember the exact moment I heard *3 Feet High and Rising*. My cousin in Indianapolis had it, and he recorded me a copy on cassette tape (well, technically he recorded Side A, but you can read more about that in the first volume of the Boom Bap Review). I listened to that tape on the car ride back to Evansville, IN, where I'm from. Then, I listened to that album at home, constantly, every day for months. I couldn't get enough of it. I had heard and enjoyed Hip-Hop music up to that point in my life, but this was different. That tape had a profound impact on my life.

Looking back, I think that album really inspired me to say yes and explore artistically. It was that album that made me want to make music. When a neighbor across the street had a garage sale and had some old, dusty drums for $15, I needed them. I needed them so I too could make some beats like De La Soul. When friends of mine were also getting into Hip-Hop, we just had to form a group. We had to come up with creative songs and skits like *3 Feet High...* Later in life, when my buddy Wonder Brown said we should go on tour and neither of us knew anything about touring, I knew we had to do it. We had to create experiences for people just like *3 Feet* created a music experience for me that I'll never forget and always go back to.

While we are talking about going back, let's go back. After I played out that *3 Feet High* tape, I was introduced to another

Native Tongue album, *Peoples...* by A Tribe Called Quest. WHAT!!!??? There was another group similar to De La Soul? A group that was just as dope, just as fresh, and had similar artistic sensibilities? But this album was different. It wasn't full of skits. It was more about the music, and that music was amazing. Then I learned about Jungle Brothers, then Black Sheep. Later, I would piece it all together with Monie Love and Queen Latifah, and I would become one of the collective's biggest fans.

But it didn't stop with the original core members. It expanded. Brand Nubian pops up on one of my favorite albums of all time, *The Low End Theory*. Phife is featured on the Fu-Schnickens debut. Chi-Ali is on *A Wolf in Sheep's Clothing*. Shortie No Mass is divine on my favorite album of all time, *Buhloone Mindstate*. Then comes *Stakes Is High*, reinforcing my love for Common and introducing me to Truth Enola and Mos Def (Yasiin Bey today). Trugoy the Dove spits a verse on Camp Lo's debut album so I have to love that. It just keeps going. Prince Paul tags Breeze Brewin to be the star on *A Prince Among Thieves*, so now he is one of my favorites. Mos and Talib come together as *Black Star*, and that is amazing. The Roots talk about how they are inspired by De La Soul, so you know I have to check them out. I do and absolutely love what they are bringing. Did I say it keeps going? It does.

It has never stopped. To this day, when I hear an album that has something special about it, something fresh that draws me in, I usually think, "This reminds me of the Native Tongues." This collective is a springboard for creativity. They have been inspiring me and countless others for over three decades now. That springboard hasn't lost any of its spring either. Today, there are artists releasing new music that has a similar feel; music that processes an Afrocentric vibe coupled with originality. Artists like Blu, Skyzoo, Sa-Roc, TH.III.RD, Little Brother, Rapsody, Oddisee, yU, and the list goes on and on and on.

Just the other day, a friend on Facebook asked if I could name a recent album that resembles the simplistic production style of

The Low End Theory, breakbeat-driven drums with standup bass lines and sparse sampling. One album came to mind immediately, *Words to the Wise* by Vic Monroe and Tone Spliff. At face value, this album is vastly different from *Low End*. However, when I go below the surface, I hear similarities. I hear that Native essence in the drums, the bass, the instrumentation, and subject matter. It is very different yet held together by a similar aesthetic.

I hear that Native Tongue influence often, and I am trying to add on to it. I've been creating music one way or another since months after I heard *3 Feet High and Rising* and have no plans in letting up. I'm making beats and working with the team at Everybody's Hip-Hop Label daily. If it weren't for the Native Tongues, I'm not sure I'd be pursuing these Hip-Hop endeavors. Perhaps I would be. One thing is for certain—the Native Tongues Collective continues to inspire me more than any other artist or group. For me, it's 3 feet high and still rising.

CHAPTER TWENTY-SEVEN

Ode to Phife Dawg from A Tribe Called Quest

Written by Joe November

Mr. Energetic, who me sound pathetic? When's the last time you heard a funky diabetic?

- Phife Dawg, "Oh My God"

I was 29 years old when I was diagnosed with Type 1 diabetes. At the time, I was stationed overseas in the US Air Force, and a random drug urinalysis test indicated high levels of glucose in my body. I was just as shocked as the Danish physician who gave me the news (note: I was stationed at Thule Air Base in Greenland, and since Greenland is home ruled by Denmark, there were Danish personnel on base along with Americans, Greenlanders, and some Canadians.) I was in great shape, worked out regularly and didn't have a history of Type 1 in the family. The news was devastating to say the least; I was forced to medically retire from the only job I had and loved, and my future was uncertain.

During this time of uncertainty, I often retreated to vibing out to my music while playing video games (hey, I was unemployed, so I had that kind of time!), and I always found myself going back to my favorite Hip-Hop group of all time: A Tribe Called Quest. ATCQ was responsible for me falling in love with Hip-Hop with their classic sophomore album, *The Low End Theory*. Jazz samples over banging boom bap beats were not new at the time, but what made this album so definitive for me was how well Q-Tip oozed his charisma and how fly Phife was lyrically.

I felt these attributes shined especially well on their follow-up LP, *Midnight Marauders*. Phife's verse on "Oh My God" resonated with me, and here is where I make my main point. The line I quoted at the beginning of this ode gave me hope during a dark time in my life. It was as if he were saying to me, "Get up man. Find some energy to move forward. I don't sound pathetic, and you shouldn't either. I accept my fate as a diabetic and you know what, you ain't never heard anyone as funky as me on the mic so you go out there and keep that same energy!" This 'throwaway' line that even he forgot he dropped was a calling to people like me – people whose bodies had failed them in some way but found a way forward despite it all.

On top of all this, Phife Dawg was a certified sports head (especially when it came to hoops!). I grew up in the 80s in Central Kentucky, and basketball was and still is my favorite sport to play and watch. Especially college hoops – I mean c'mon, I spent my entire childhood rooting for one of the most storied programs in college basketball: the University of Kentucky Wildcats. Who can forget the '92 NCAA East Regional Final between Kentucky and Duke, where Christian Laettner miraculously hit what was forever known as "The Shot" to win the game in overtime and propel the Blue Devils to the Final Four? I'd like to, but I digress. Anyway, I saw that same love for basketball in Phife, too. Remember him rocking that Seton Hall jersey in the "Check The Rhime" video (s/o to Pookey Wigington)? Remember him sporting a Georgia Tech Yellow Jackets hat in arguably one of the greatest posse cuts of all time, "Scenario?" And who can forget Phife spitting his "Electric Relaxation" verse in New York City's Square Diner while in a North Carolina Tar Heels hoodie? His sports references go on and on. He certainly wasn't the first rapper to wear basketball gear and slide hoops references in his rhymes, but to me he was the most memorable to do it. It was just who he was, and I admired that.

At the time of this writing, Phife's posthumous album *Forever* was released this week. It's a solid album, full of notable features from talented artists. One track stood out to me the most. In "God Send" feat. Dwele, Phife opened up about his struggle with diabetes in a way I had never heard before. It was raw, honest, and sincere to the core. There was a cautionary undertone to his storytelling that makes me reevaluate how I'm managing my disease. To this end, we celebrate his life, but it's sad to realize that we will probably never hear Mutty Ranks drop more music for his fans. We'll never see a full-fledged Native Tongues Reunion tour with all the core members on one stage. Phife took his role in Hip-Hop seriously, and it's unfortunate that diabetes took him away from us. I know I can't be the only Hip-Hop head who looks at his legacy and is reminded about how fragile life is. On "2 Live Forever", he ended his monologue by saying, "let's get it together." So let's get it together y'all… for Phife. Rest In Power.

CHAPTER TWENTY-EIGHT

The Incredible Pieces of Phife

Written by iomos marad and Jason Cuthbert

Phife's Catchy Intro Bars

Jason: When A Tribe Called Quest entered into 1991 with *The Low End Theory*, that second album became my favorite Tribe project because, along with that dynamic production and Q-Tip's poetic wizardry, we really got to witness Phife Dawg step it up like crazy. Phife not only appeared on more songs and got his own solo on there with "Butter", but his confidence cut through those incredible jazzy soundscapes, knocking drums, and booming bass.

iomos: I thought I was the only person who saw Phife in that light. I thought Phife was solid on *People's Instinctive Travels and the Paths of Rhythm*, especially his "Can I Kick It" verse and the verse he dropped on "Ham and Eggs." His verses may not have been stellar at that time, but I remember I definitely gravitated to him and knew he had potential. But you are absolutely right. When that *Low End Theory* dropped, Phife came in like: HERE I AM. Like Ali said in the Tribe Documentary, "In making *The Low End Theory,* there's definitely, you know, what I think is evident to everyone and that's the emergence of Phife Diggy Dawg." I agree with Ali. Phife became Phife on *Low End*. I remember getting so excited to hear DJ

Premier cutting Phife's voice saying, *"Now here's a funky introduction,"* to kick off Gangstarr's *Hard to Earn* album at the beginning of "Alongwaytogo." I heard a Hip-Hop artist say that there is no greater honor to have Preemo cut your voice for a hook on a song. I'm so glad that Phife was honored in that way.

Jason: True Indeed, "Can I Kick It" definitely had that energy that Phife expanded on further with the sophomore album. Even on a classic posse cut like "Scenario" with Leaders of the New School, where we still talk about that standout Busta Rhymes explosion, I still can feel Phife's ferocious presence when he set his verse off with:

> *Heyo, Bo knows this, and Bo knows that / But Bo don't know jack, 'cause Bo can't rap.* ("Scenario", *The Low End Theory*, 1991)

In that early 90s era, thanks to Nike commercials and a two-sport career playing MLB baseball for the Kansas City Royals and NFL football with the Los Angeles Raiders, Bo Jackson was like the biggest sports star after Michael Jordan (ironically another dual-sport king). But that didn't stop Phife from poking his chest out and proclaiming that being an all-star on that microphone was bigger than the World Series and the Super Bowl put together.

iomos: *"So what do you know/ The Di-Dawg is first up to bat/ No batteries included/ and no strings attached"* Man, bro. The first time I heard that line, I was like, *Yeah Phife! Let's go! It's time!!!* I felt that way the first time I heard him breathe on "Buggin Out." And then when he had a chance to shine on his own on "Butter", it was obvious that Phife had been putting in work with his pen. I remember reading an article in *The Source* that Phife was spending a lot of time with Busta Rhymes before the making of *Low End*. I don't know if that had anything to do with it, but regardless of what it was, I'm glad that Phife was going to get the props that he deserved. "Butter" and "8 Million Stories" are two of my favorite songs in Hip-Hop, and it has been debated on which one is better. For me, I love the transparency and storytelling of "8 Million Stories."

Sticking Up for the Underdogs

iomos: I think it is important for me to mention that I always side with the under-dawg members of certain groups. Like, for example, The Roots. I always gravitated to Malik B as an emcee the same way I gravitated to Phife. And it's crazy to think that two of my favorite emcees of all time who mean so much to me have made their transition, and they both carry the Arabic name Malik, which means "owner" or "King." Two owners and kings who were considered the sidekicks of their groups but owned their positions within their respective groups and now are considered kings within Hip-Hop. Or at least I see them in that light, if that means anything (laughing).

Jason: Bro, I never even thought about that comparison to Malik B. You are on point with that! They may not always make the Top MC lists like Black Thought and Q-Tip, but their presence was needed, and they added balance and were both really relatable. I can't believe we lost both of those brothers when they were only in their 40s.

The sense of urgency that Malik "Phife Dawg" Taylor was rocking made him somebody who was trying to grab your attention with the first bar of his verses. He wasn't trying to be ignored with opening lines like:

> *Now here's a funky introduction of how nice I am / Tell your mother, tell your father, send a telegram.* ("Check the Rhime," *The Low End Theory*, 1991)

> *I like 'em brown, yellow, Puerto Rican or Haitian / Name is Phife Dawg from the Zulu Nation.* ("Electric Relaxation," *Midnight Marauders*, 1993)

iomos: Bruh. That is a really solid perspective. Now that you mentioned this, I can see the sense of urgency and energy behind his rhymes and his delivery. Even the tone of Phife's voice in contrast to Q-Tip was definitely a higher, more hyper toned pitch, which made a beautiful symmetry between the two of them. It's also interesting to note that his name *Phife* might have been derived from the English word *fife* which is *a small high-pitched flute similar to a piccolo; that has a shrill tone and is used chiefly to accompany drums in a marching band.* This makes so much sense now. My imagination takes me to a young Malik trying to think of a name that fits his personality and his unique vocal tones and him coming across this word and him saying, "this is who I am going to be over the drums that Q-Tip and Ali produce for our group. But I can't just write it with an "f." Phife was moved to do what Hip-Hop is known to do with the English language for time. He changed the "f" in fife to "ph" and the legacy of "The Five Foot Assassin" begins.

Honest and Transparent About Who He Is

Jason: Another thing I respected about what Phife brought to Tribe was his blunt honesty. He had no problem telling you that lyrically he was the *"five foot assassin,"* standing at 5'3" in height in his *"size 8 Adidas,"* because he knew he had the heart of a giant. Phife wasn't afraid to let you know he was the "funky diabetic," putting his personal health issues right in the music, turning something traumatic into a title of distinction. How about when he said:

> *(Damn Phife, you got fat!) / Yeah, I know it looks pathetic / Ali Shaheed Muhammad got me doing calisthenics.* ("The Chase Pt. II", *Midnight Marauders*, 1993)

Also, by me being of Trinidadian descent, Phife made me feel a whole lot of pride when he proclaimed:

> *Trini gladiator, anti-hesitator / Shaheed push the fader from here to Grenada.* ("Oh My God", *Midnight Marauders*, 1993)

iomos: Yes, indeed. Honesty and transparency are the main things that I loved about Phife and a few other Native Tongue members. I gravitated to Phife, Tribe, De La and Native Tongues for this very reason because growing up on the South Side of Chicago where gang culture and involvement was a way of life, Phife and the other Native Tongue members—Posdnous comes to mind whenever the word transparency and emceeing comes up for me—were giving me permission and saying it was okay to be yourself and be who you are. I love that Phife had the courage to embrace and express who he was as a Trinidadian battling with juvenile diabetes (as his beautiful mother Cheryl Boyce-Taylor described in the Tribe doc). I think it was a way of saying to the world, *even if you see me on Yo! MTV Raps or a late-night show performing, I still deal with the issues and problems that* *come with living life just like you.* This is why Phife will always be a giant and bigger than life to me despite his 5-foot-3 frame and size 8 shoes that no one will be able to fill now or later. Phife said it best, *"I wear New Balance sneakers to avoid a narrow path/ mess around with this and catch the size of 'em."* In my opinion, there are two giants within the legacy of Hip-Hop; Andre the Giant of Showbiz & AG (DITC) and Phife Diggy Dawg. Hands down.

Jason: I felt the exact same way about Native Tongues. Growing up in Rochester, New York, a much smaller city than Chicago, fitting in was a common approach to gain acceptance and avoid getting clowned or bullied when you are young. But I didn't have it in me to dress, look, and think like everyone, and A Tribe Called Quest, De La Soul, and Black Sheep were that blueprint to be me.

Sports Jerseys and Sneaker Culture

Jason: I may not follow professional sports as much as I used to in the 80s and 90s, but Phife's love of sports made him stand out a lot to me, especially with all those witty sports references, his pride for his New York Knicks, his New York Jets, his New York Yankees/Mets and his North Carolina Tarheels. I might be wrong, but does Phife Dawg have the most sports-related bars in Hip-Hop?

iomos: I would agree 100%, my brother. I don't think there is any other emcee who has more sports-related bars in Hip-Hop. In the Tribe Doc, I love how Jarobi shared about Phife and their bond over *sports-related activities* and how he spoke to everybody knowing about Phife being a sports enthusiast (laughing). It is no wonder why Phife was injecting his love for sports into his rhymes. You can tell that Jarobi's statement is true in the line of "8 Million Stories" when Phife said, *"Where the hell can Nicky be I'm going to (you know) her up/ I got two tickets for the Knicks and she cold stood me up."* This line further confirms Phife's life revolving around sports-related activities, even down to taking a girlfriend to a Knicks game (laughing). I remember when I saw Tribe at the House of Blues in Chicago (I don't remember what year it was). Phife came out in a sweet #34 Walter Payton Jersey with some fresh Nikes on that I had never seen before. It was always this homage that Phife had for sports and athletes. I was so glad to see how ESPN embraced Phife for being the sports enthusiast that he is. And it was dope when ESPN's Scott Van Pelt did a segment on Phife showing his gratitude and respect for Phife.

Jason: He was like the ultimate sports commentator (iomos nodding head in agreement):

> *With all these trials and tribulations, yo, I've been affected / And to top it off, (John) Starks got ejected.* ("8 Million Stories", *Midnight Marauders*, 1993)

> *Large Professor in the house, you know how we do / I skate on your crew, like Mario Lemieux.* ("Keep It Rollin'", *Midnight Marauders*, 1993)

> *I'm prompt with my business and I do things on the double / Yo, I'm out like Buster Douglas, I say peace to MC Trouble.* ("Vibes and Stuff", *The Low End Theory*, 1991)

Jason: Plus, let's not forget that Phife's athletic fashion was way ahead of the throw-back jersey and fitted cap phase of the early to mid-2000s that Fabolous, Jay-Z, Clipse, Kanye West, Jadakiss, and Cam'ron were known for. Phife made it cool to rock an athletic dress code in his 1990s music videos.

iomos: Yes, indeed. I went and got a Bears jersey with my name on the back of it because of Phife's expression of sportswear. Break it down for the people, J.

Jason: "Check the Rhyme" - Seton Hall (NCAA) basketball jersey & Cleveland Indians (MLB) baseball jersey and cap

"Scenario" - Georgia Tech Yellow Jackets (NCAA) cap, San Jose Sharks (NHL) cap, Seattle Supersonics (NBA) cap

"Jazz (We've Got)/Buggin' Out" - Georgia Tech Yellow Jackets Starter jacket

"Electric Relaxation" - North Carolina Tar Heels (NCAA) hoodie

"Oh My God" - New Jersey Devils (NHL) hockey jersey customized with "Phife" on the back and the number "5" for his alias, the Five-Footer.

DJ Rasta Root, who was Phife's close friend, DJ, manager, and business partner, spoke about Phife's gear game in a piece for *Inside Hook* where he states Phife enjoyed shopping in Philadelphia's Mitchell and Ness:

> He didn't care what he spent on a jersey. He'd buy a jersey based on a person's career, rather than the jersey having an interesting colorway.

iomos: Wow! Thanks for sharing this. See. This speaks to his level of sports knowledge. I love how he was breaking down his *5 favorite little men in NBA History* (Kenny Anderson, Mark Jackson, Kenny "The Jet" Smith, Allen Iverson, and Chris Paul) in the Tribe doc and, if you notice, 3 out of the 5 point guards Phife mentioned are from New York.

Self-Deprecating Sense of Humor

Jason: Phife was straight up hilarious with his punchlines - funny without being a joke. He was like that stand-up comic that gets on stage and roasts anybody in the front row that he feels is slacking in some way. But he would even make fun of himself, like The Notorious B.I.G. would about his weight...

iomos: Color and looks. *"Black and ugly as ever, however"* (laughing)

Jason: ...It felt to me like Phife was good at using his humor as self-therapy, fully aware of what you might think of him, and letting you know he doesn't care. Like the man said,

> *I never let a statue tell me how nice I am.*
> ("Award Tour", *Midnight Marauders*, 1993)

Loving ourselves is hard to accomplish in a society that acts like our skin color and socio-economic status are problems. Although I never had the pleasure to meet the brother Phife, let me speak to his spirit right now and say, thank you for inspiring the confidence and self-respect that is needed to survive out here, so we can be better than we have been treated and treat others with the dignity they deserve.

iomos: Well said, bro. I also love the line on the song "Word Play" off that *Beats, Rhymes & Life* album when Phife said:

> *Analyze/ that's what I do to emcees/ that be talkin bout they this and that/ money please/ Ego/ I'm on my own jock still/ Cause if I don't say I'm the best tell me who the hell will*

This line embodies and reinforces your train of thought around us being able to love ourselves within a society that acts like our skin color and socio-economic status are a problem. Love him or hate him, Talib said it best on the "Knowledge of Self" song on the *Black Star* album, *"No question. Being a Black man is demanding."* It is demanding because the pro-Euro colonial structure of society was designed to reject, exclude, and tear us down. Phife demonstrates so masterfully the ability to walk that fine line of being humble and self-deprecating while also being confident and championing who we are ourselves. I'm loving this conversation, bruh. What else do you want to build on?

Hip-Hop Purist

Jason: For better or for worse, Malik "Phife" Taylor made it known that he didn't want his Hip-Hop music watered down, and commercialized rappers clearly got the man vexed with their repetitive zombie music. He had harsh words for R&B-ish rappers, seemingly the entire sub-genre of New Jack Swing, cats that glamorized gun-toting, and men that abused women. Phife had a very hard line when it came to his dignity, and he refused to lower his standards. Even on Phife's posthumous album, he was man enough to make amends and apologize for infidelity and strained relationships with A Tribe Called Quest—spoken like a true Family Man, and a man of the people who cuts the "e" off the end of "Fame" and puts his "Fam" before "Fame."

iomos: Yo! That is an excellent point. And that line right there says it all, bruh. I feel like Phife might have taken a play on words out of Posdnous' book with that one. Another thing I would like to mention about Phife as a Hip-Hop Purist was his ability to stand up for the voiceless and the powerless. I love how Phife always seemed to use his platform to stand up and speak out against things he did not agree with despite the consequences or aftermath that could have come with those statements. You remember lines like:

> *Imma negro/ He's a negro want to be a negro too/ but beating on a girl is something that a puss would do/ I love jazz but that doesn't mean I'm timid/ Not really a gangsta rap but I can swing it for a minute* ("Jazz (We've Got) Remix", *The Low End Theory*, 1991) — This line was in response to the news of Denise Dee Barnes being brutally beaten up by Dr. Dre.

Or,

> *I'm all into my music cuz that's how I make papes/ Tryin' to make hits like Kid Capri makes tapes/ Me sweat another? I do my own thing/ strictly hardcore tracks not a new jack swing* ("Jazz (We've Got) Remix", *The Low End Theory*, 1991)

This line feels like Phife was prophetically seeing that the culture we all love so much was beginning to change/ morph/ or evolve into something that was not true to the sound and aesthetic of boom bap Hip-Hop. Or even

> *Hey yo swing swing swing, to chop chop chop/ Yo that's the sound when MCs get mopped/Don't come around town without the hip in your hop/ Cause when the sh— hits the fan, that a—'ll get dropped/ MC's want to attack me but them punks can't cope/ I'll have you left without a job, like Isaac from The Love Boat* ("Keep It Rollin'", *Midnight Marauders, 1993)*

Phife represents what a Hip-Hop purist means down to the very essence of his being. A true emcee who might not have liked his voice but knew not to fight the fans because we all were waiting with anticipation to hear the clever catchy bars; ready to defend the underdog with honest and transparent genius, sports-related, self-deprecating with a sense of humor lines to keep the pure essence of Hip-Hop fire burning.

This is dedicated to: Phife, Phife Dawg, The Phifer, Phife Diggy, The Five-Foot Assassin, The Five-Footer, Malik The Five-Foot Freak, The Funky Diabetic, Dynomutt, Mutty Ranks, The Trini-Gladiator, Don Juice, & Dr. Pepper who will be forever missed but can never be replaced. From Jason Cuthbert & iomos marad. Peace & Solidarity.

CHAPTER TWENTY-NINE

Why Posdnous is the Best

Written by iomos marad and agreed upon by MC Till

I was born in the Boogie Down catscan
Where my building fell down on the rats and
People sold the super on a trip to the penile (penile)
While I settle off the shores of the Long Isle
("Breakadawn", *Buhloone Mindstate*, 1993)

Out of the heavens August one-seven, sixty-nine
Born I, Wondah Why
with the thoughts to rhyme
Till there was no longer thoughts to dream
When an unpolished demo led to limos at the age of eighteen
Accompanied by the screams, Plug One
Shot up with fame like novacaine it made me numb
So numb I wouldn't been able to feel
N***** diggin in my pockets for my currency reels
But still, I make girls brown eyes blue at will
(until)
My a— was no longer mass appeal
Oh sh*t, I guess that was all the fame I was allotted
Wait a minute, new video, like a leopard I'm spotted
In a night club chillin' with Khalil and Phife
I be that farmer cultivating owning acres of mics
And I likes to make it known Strong Island stylin'
For a while, so do that dance
("Wonce Again Long Island", *Stakes Is High*, 1996)

One of my favorite emcees of all time was born in the Bronx but was raised in West Amityville (known now as East Massapequa) located within the Town of Oyster Bay in Nassau County on the South Shore of Long Island in NYC. *When he fell out of the heavens* through the womb of his mother on August 17, 1969, he was named Kelvin Mercer but became known to the world as *Posdnous* aka *Pos* aka *Plug Won* aka *Plug Wondah Why* aka *Wondah Why* aka *Workmatic* aka *Mercenary* aka *Mad Mad Merce from the De La*—Soul that is.

Who is your favorite emcee of all time? Who are your top 5 emcees of all time? Who are your top 10 emcees of all time? These questions are asked all the time within Hip-Hop circles. It's funny when you think about it because these questions are being asked only to determine what category you should be placed in. Are you a *true Hip-Hop Head* or are you just a *Hip-Hop/Rap by-stander* who only knows the names of a few popular rap artists who can only be found in pop mainstream media platforms?

Anyway, you should already know one of my answers to these questions based on the title of this article, but just to be clear, KRS-One and Posdnous are my favorite emcees of all time. When I think about this, it's crazy because most people can accept the KRS-One answer, but when I utter the name Posdnous, I often get strange looks and silence and receive responses like *"Posda-who? Say that again? Why him?"* Well, here is the perfect opportunity for me to explain to you all why Posdnous is one of my favorite emcees of all time.

I have had what seems to be a lifetime to really ponder and reflect on building my defense. So for me to explain my thoughts clearly, I broke it down into four categories for you all to follow along: (1) *It's All in the Name*; (2) *Tha Voice*; (3) *Transparency through Rhymes*, and (4) *The Complex art of Speak = Dope lyrical content*.

(1) IT'S ALL IN THE NAME

Every great emcee has a dope name, and Posdnous is no different. I often think about why Kelvin Mercer chose to use *sound sop* spelled backward to be his name to emcee? But once you break it down, you can only say that Mercer is pure genius for coming up with his emcee calling card.

> *No longer Kelvin Mercer but the Posdnuos—Plug One*
> *Yo I found fun in the scribblin' of speak on a naked white sheet*
> *Most recognized by my dark brown self*
> *Yo you found some wealth?*
> *More in my mind than in my pocket*
> *But I's got every Girbaud that ever sagged*
> *I met some hoes, met some girls*
> *Did a tour that took me all around the world*

("En Focus", *Buhloone Mindstate*, 1993)

Sop spelled backwards (*Pos*) + *sound* spelled backward *(dnous)* creates the name *Posdnous*. The word *Sop* means *a gift* or a thing given or done as a concession of no great value to appease someone whose main concerns or demands are not being met (which I interpret to mean being the voice for the voiceless). SOP as an acronym can stand for Sounds Of Power. The human voice is an instrument that can project sounds of power because life and death is in the power of the tongue. I would argue that Posdnous chooses to use his voice as a gift to project sounds of power to bring life to anyone who chooses to listen. I think Pos would agree with my train of thought based on him saying things like:

> *I'm the most from the coast of the East, then flee*
> *Droppin more knowledge than litter, on the New York pave*
> *It's me, Wondah Why, in the place to be*

Certified, as superior, MC
While others explore to make it hardcore
I make it hard for, wack MCs to even step inside the door
'Cause these kids is rhyming, sometimey
And when we get to racing on the mic, they line up to see
The lyrical killing, with stained egos on the ceiling
My rhymes escalates like Black death rates
Over music plates, being played as the rule
Kids thinking stepping to the Soul, you're labeled fools
Who claims to drop jewels but for now you do the catching
I don't worry on what crew you run, or what section of Earth
You reside, you're not even a man
So I don't deem it mandatory taking your pride
But I will, cause my man said Soul for the life
You cried "Keepin it real", yet you should try keepin it right
That's understanding microphone mathematics
Which leaves the currency in temporary world status
And when one shows he posed threat to this one
This one will make that one into none
Simple equation, zero, you shouldn't play hero
If you can't stand Strong like the Island I'm from

("The Bizness", *Stakes Is High*, 1996)

Pos chooses to use his God-given lyrical abilities to give listeners the gift of life instead of being a fool with his gift to speak. Again, I would argue that Pos being one of my favorite emcees begins and ends with his name.

(2) THA VOICE

Guru of the legendary Gangstarr (Rest In Power) said it best:

> *It's mostly tha voice, that gets you up*
> *It's mostly tha voice, that makes you buck*
> *A lot of rappers got flavor, and some got skills*
> *But if your voice ain't dope then you need to [chill... chill...]*

("Mostly Tha Voice", *Hard To Earn*, 1994)

Ask any emcee; it all starts with the voice, and it's no different with Pos who has a unique voice and vocal tone that is distinct only to him. It's just like when you hear Guru, you know it's Guru. When you hear Pos, you know it's Pos on the mic breathing sounds of power to get you to see the world a bit different than you did before hearing him rhyme.

(3) TRANSPARENCY THROUGH RHYMES

One of the things I love most about Posdnous is how transparent he is about his life through rhymes. Many might perceive or take these rare characteristics of vulnerability and transparency as a sign of weakness. I completely disagree with this sentiment. In fact, I believe there is a strength in being vulnerable and revealing everyday truths about your life and by doing that, it creates three amazing things; (1) it brings you closer to the emcee/artist; (2) it speaks to the humanity of the artist, and; (3) it allows the listener to be in community with the artist. I would argue that there are only a few emcees who embody this characteristic, and Posdnous is definitely one of them. When I listen to Pos, I feel connected to him because I realize he is going through the same struggles of life that I go through, even though those struggles might not be identical. Let's dive into the transparency of Pos through his own words:

> *I recall kissin on my lady, talkin bout makin babies*

> *Now we made the baby, but cannot connect as legal spouses*
> *Now me and my daughter reside in different houses*
> *What louses up the structure, is leavin things up to*
> *The child lesser, than a child runnin wild from mild pressure*
> *Mega (mega) nega (nega) tive*
> *To live a master plan when that plan has no master*
> *You stare at false tongues, leadin the yung'un to disaster*
> ("Pony Ride", *Stakes Is High*, 1996)

You can really see Pos' transparency in the lyrics above, but it is even stronger on the song "I Am I Be" on the *Buhloone Mindstate* album when he says things like:

> *I am Posdnous*
> *I be the new generation of slaves*
> *Here to make papes to buy a record exec rakes*
> *The pile of revenue I create*
> *But I guess I don't get a cut 'cause my rent's a month late*
>
> *Look ma, no protection*
> *Now I got a daughter named Ayana Monay*
> *And I can play the cowboy to rustle in the dough*
> *So the scenery is healthy where her eyes lay*
> *I am an early bird but the feathers are black*
> *So the apples that I catch are usually all worms*
> *But it's a must to decipher one's queen*
> *From a worm who plays groupie and spread around the bad germ*
> *Faker than a fist of kids*
> *Speakin' that they're Black*
> *When they're just n***** trying to be Greek*

Or some tongues who lied
And said "We'll be natives to the end"
Nowadays we don't even speak
I guess we got our own life to live
Or is it because we want our own kingdom to rule?
Every now and then I step to the now
For now I see back then I might have acted like a fool
Now I won't apologize for it
This is not a bunch of Bradys
But a bunch of black man's pride
("I Am I Be", *Buhloone Mindstate*, 1993)

I hope I'm proving my point as the transparency and truth of Pos's rhymes are ringing out from these stanzas of lines from someone who I consider to be a great literary poet, lyricst, and emcee. To all the young folks who might be reading this and desire to become artists, emcees/ rappers, it is completely okay to reveal who you really are as a human being and be vulnerable through your words. Follow the lead of Posdnous.

(4) The Complex art of Speak = Dope lyrical content

We seem to be living in a season and time where it appears to be cool for rappers to carry and express a hard, hyper-masculine (which many people might label as toxic) presenting content through the art of rhyming that expresses the message, *if you expletive with me, I can end your life*. Which speaks to my final point about Posdnous' complex art of speaking. In his own words, Pos said:

I been stylin' abstract since loose leafs was the sh-t
Catch me breathin' on planes where the gangsta's outdated
F-ck being hard, Posdnuos is complicated

("In the Woods", *Buhloone Mindstate*, 1993)

Here comes a brother hipping others on the style they lack
I've always rhymed abstract, I even know the brother named Abstract
I am the earner of the soul in mine
Forget the physical cause the physical will die with time
I'm shaped to vibrate in definite proportions
Of the kids who need the fix (Just listen to the mix)
I got the knowledge constant non-stop for the rubbishing
Like (n*****) use the Clinton loops as if they owned the publishing
Gums be bleeding from illegal feeding on my verb
I bring the Mardi Gras to your face
I outwit vipers in my rhyme cipher
I can easily lick them 'cause they're victims of the subconscious race

("She Fe MCs", *Clear Lake Auditorium EP*, 1994)

It sniffs good
Punks show disguises when I'm standing in the wood
I be the in cause the brother holdin' Glocks is out
I be the in cause the pusher runnin' blocks is out
I be the in cause the kid smokin' weed
Shootin' seed which leads to a girl's stomach
Being 'bout a half a ton is out
Show the finger print and give me good grief for my lumber
Pants will sag cause my license as a plumber

Feel the Plug (yo, something's wrong here)
Now give a shout
("Eye Patch", *Buhloone Mindstate*, 1993)

Pos' main objective as an emcee is the opposite of being tough and hardcore (even though De La Soul is by no means soft in any way). Pos does not have to express hyper-masculinity through toughness because his lyrics are tough enough. Pos' lyrics are so complex that you would have to engage in an art that seems to be no longer popular. Listen. You have to really listen to catch the jewels and gems of what Pos is dropping with every verse. This could not be more evident than on the song "Down Syndrome" on the *Stakes Is High* album. Pos blacks out lyrically and continues to demonstrate why his rhymes are so complex:

I be that mind blessin blessin these lessons we've ignited
Want to bring it to my face man you're cordially invited
cause I've cited, you possess no science in your thinking
So I'm gonna (never) you're blinking

I'm Plug One-of-a-kind, for you people's delight
And for you sucker MCs, step to your knees
Ain't no second thoughts and all your thoughts are from Orion
I can tell that you a devil by them rhymes you're designin'
Your play doggin tactics can't f-ck with my facets
Just because you talk all that glock sh-t don't mean you can rock sh-t!

Let me tell you a little something about Soul (tell em son)
I be a piece of the East coast, so give a toast to

> *Plug Wonder Why back in the day who soaked his words in ginger*
> *So when I ran a phrase in June you didn't catch it til December*
> *I'm a member of them kids from the inner city*
> *Giving you kitties audible treats, you be aching for making*
> *More money than a pagan holiday*
> *Not from the PJs, yet I still got something to say*
> ("Down Syndrome", *Stakes Is High*, 1996)

What more can I say about the dopeness of the great Posdnous who is most definitely a Super Emcee, moving through the culture and the music industry unassuming as Clark Kent (forgive me for the DC reference to all the Marvel lovers like me out there). Pos' rhymes move faster than a speeding thought and are able to leap over sky scraping mainstream rap artist(s) with a single line? One of his biggest strengths of complexity is his play on words. I love how he plays with words to make the listener dig deeper into listening and thinking intently:

> *Aye yo, Aye yo, Aye yo, ain't nothin' street about me*
> *more like a light post*
> *Shinin' above all*
> *who are y'all to boast*
> *Stayed calm when harm came to me to host*
>
> *My vocab grabs many, long to cultivate raps*
> *It's gettin' filled moms jack penny*
> *used to be unknown around the way*
> *Now my biz became a bouquet*
> *Every nose in it*
> *fillin' up seats like a session in a Senate*
> *Been a minute since ya heard the souls*

So the soul gon' cost ya three
All ya people want to front like the soul don't hold control
But it don't mean sh-t to me
("Watch Out", *AOI: Bionix*, 2001)

I got status 'cause I'm baddest with the paint
Giving upside down frowns to London wood 703
Her moms didn't like it, I had to let be
For the fact I lays bricks
'Cause my semen ends with the letter T
My seed is hard to submerge
("Area", *Buhloone Mindstate*, 1993)

While you others represent, I present my rep
Cause when it comes to making dents, I'm that main in print
Even smoked from blunts which give eyes the reddish tint
Could not prevent, you from seeing I'm the light

Send your tattered a– home, with celly phones I roam
With my fleet, here to make this rap game complete
While you live fables, unstable, acting very radical
Projecting like you're hard, when in fact you're quite vaginal
("Supaemcees", *Stakes Is High*, 1996)

    After reading and dissecting Pos' lyrics it makes me long for the days when emcees took time writing their rhymes and making sure their lyrics were high IQ. I don't know what else there is for me to say but Posdnous is like one of those classic old body GM (General Motors) cars that are no longer being manufactured. Pos is a dope emcee built from the ground up beginning with his name, his voice, the transparency of his rhymes, and his complex art of speech that equals dope lyrical content that I believe is unmatched. Pos does not get the props he deserves as an emcee, but I hope this article will balance the scales a bit. Peace.

CHAPTER THIRTY

Bob Power

Written by iomos marad

Yo, my mic is sounding bug. Bob Power, you there? (Yeah)
Adjust the bass and treble make my sh-t sound clear (echo)

("The Chase Pt. II" from *Midnight Marauders*)

Bob Power is an important name to mention regarding the foundation of sound, audio texture, and sonic vibrations that drew many of us critical listeners to become fans of the Native Tongue sound.

Although Bob Power would probably admit that a lot of what he did (and still does now) was experimental, he has used his imagination as a song arranger, engineer, mixer, producer, programmer, and musician to enhance the sound of Hip-Hop legends in the game such as *Stetsasonic, A Tribe Called Quest, Common, Da Bush Babees, De La Soul, Fu-Schnickens, Jungle Brothers, Killah Priest, Main Source, Organized Konfusion, Rahzel, The Roots, Run DMC, and Slum Village* just to name a few.

Not to mention that he has worked with artists outside of Hip-Hop such as *Brand New Heavies, Bob James, Chaka Khan, Erykah Badu, Indie.Arie, Meshell Ndegeocello, Miles Davis, and Tony!, Toni!, Toné!* The mentioning of these artists is a way of demonstrating just how versatile and influential Bob Power is within and outside of the genre and culture of Hip-Hop.

Bob Power's story begins in Chicago where he was born and raised before moving to Rye, New York. He eventually moved to St. Louis, Missouri to attend Webster College where he studied music theory because he was inspired by *Buddy Guy, Otis Rush,* and *Albert King*, who were considered the great blues guitarists of the era. Bob also studied classical composition and conducting and obtained a master's degree in jazz from Lone Mountain College (which is now the University of San Francisco). Bob was scoring music for an award-winning television show on PBS called *Over Easy* while he lived in California from 1975 to 1982. Bob also contributed to advertising campaigns for a number of companies such as *The American Cancer Society* that earned him an Emmy.

"I am Bob and I am really-really tired of doing this, you guys"
("I Am I Be" from *Buhloone Mindstate* by De La Soul)

In 1982, Bob decided to move back to New York to push his music career further by performing in various venues. Bob's introduction to working with Hip-Hop artists came from a request from the owner of *Calliope Studios* asking Bob to sit in as an engineer for the legendary Hip-Hop group Stetsasonic (who many dub as the first Hip-Hop band) for their album *On Fire*. During an Okayplayer interview with Bob entitled *How Bob Put The Low End In Tribe Called Quest's* The Low End Theory, he talked about how he became "a kind of staff engineer" at Calliope and he talked about how the studio was open to Hip-Hop but not really open to the Hip-Hop cultured youth that was occupying space there to create. Bob recalls:

> Well I had been kind of a staff engineer at a place called Calliope and a lot of Hip-Hop crews came through our doors to do their thing. We were open,

we were not stuck in the old school. You know, there was a lot of sort of unconscious racism going on in the studios at that time, so — and to be fair, not so much because there were people of color coming in but more because it was 18, 19-year old kids who dressed and talked differently than these people had ever heard before. The studios in New York were fairly integrated for a long time, so the whole jazz age — the jazz way of looking and talking — had been in effect for 30 or 40 years. And then Hip-Hop was a new way — literally — of talking, walking, dressing, speaking — so we were very open to it. I met them [Tribe] midway through the first record [*People's Instinctive Travels...*] and we clicked.

I would say that Bob *clicking* with Tribe is an understatement. I see Bob and Tribe as like-minded individuals who created a life-long bond over creating music. Bob shared the same mantra and goal as Tribe which is "making good music with good people" which he credits Q-Tip, Ali, and Phife as being. This is a great mantra to have, and I bet that was a huge contributor to the creation of classic albums like *The Low End Theory* and beyond. In another interview, Bob talked about his involvement in the engineering and mixing of that album. In Bob's own words:

> *The Low End Theory* was an interesting record; in a way, it was *The Sgt. Pepper's Lonely Hearts Club Band* of Hip-Hop. It's a record that changed the way that people thought about putting music together. I'm not a big Hip-Hop historian; I just know the stuff that I worked on. Until that point, when people used samples on records, it was pretty much one loop that played throughout. With *The Low End Theory*, and *People's Instinctive Travels...* to a lesser extent, Q-Tip and Ali Shaheed were at the

leading edge of a new wave where people started making elaborate musical constructions out of samples from different places that would not, and in many ways could not, have been played by regular players."

Tribe's partnership with Bob made them pioneers of sampling that reached new heights and levels, encouraging other groups like the legendary Roots crew to take up the mantle of sampling in a new way as well. Which makes me think, would the Roots have had the courage to create *Do You Want More?* or *Illadelph Halflife* (where experimenting with sampling themselves as musicians happened) if it wasn't for the creation of *The Low End Theory*?

I flips, redder than pork, comin' to New York to mix
(It's Bob Power) With the snares and kicks to fix
    ("Distortion to Static" from *Do You Want More?!!!??!* by The Roots)

Bob Power definitely represents the bridge between the old and new school of music creation and production, not only because of his extensive music career but because of his willingness to be open-minded and try new things. What if he would have told the owner of Calliope that he didn't want to engineer? Or what if he would have told Stetsasonic, "I only work with real musicians." Thank God he didn't because we would not have many of the albums that we love and hold near and dear to our hearts. Or we would have them, but the quality of the sound would not be that good. I watched an interview with Chip Fu of the Fu-Schnickens, and he talked about the care that Bob Power had with the artists that he worked with. You can also tell that Bob was having fun in the countless sessions he did with the Native Tongues Collective. Whether he was responding to Q-Tip asking him if he's there on "Words From the Abstract" or playing the police urging the pedestrian party goers "*Alright. You guys want to move the cars. Come on. Let's go"* on "The Jam" from the *Beats, Rhymes and Life* album. Bob may have been in the background working the boards or helping out in other capacities that come with being a studio engineer, but his presence and fingerprints are on a lot of those Native Tongue projects that are certified classics.

So from the Boom Bap Chat and Everybody's Hip-Hop, we want to take the time to say thank you to the great Bob Power for not only your contribution to Hip-Hop culture but for the work you have done with one of - if not the greatest - Hip-Hop crews of all time. Much respect and love to you sir and we hope that you are grooming more engineers or artists to be like you as the Arts Professor in the Clive Davis Institute of Recorded Music at New York University's Tisch School of the Arts located in New York City, NY.

CHAPTER THIRTY-ONE

A Letter to DJ Red Alert

Written by iomos marad

Dear Uncle Red Alert,

I hope all is well with you and your family.

I have always had much respect and admiration for you, but it was when you were a guest on *Drink Champs* w/ NORE and DJ EFN that my respect and admiration for you increased. After watching that episode again to write this article about you, I had to write you this letter to let you know how much I respect you as one of my elders and teachers and mentors in Hip-Hop. And just like the brothers on Drink Champs, as a representative of Everybody's Hip-Hop Label and the Boom Bap Chat podcast I would like to take the time to give you your flowers in the form of this letter.

On the album, *White People,* by Handsome Boy Modeling School, De La Soul has a song entitled "If it Wasn't for You" where the chorus simply repeats the words *if it wasn't for you.* The words of that chorus are so fitting for you because, if it wasn't for you, the world probably would have never heard of the Jungle Brothers, A Tribe Called Quest, Black Sheep, Queen Latifah, Monie Love, and Chi Ali. I don't know how many fans of Native Tongues know how much you mean to Hip-Hop culture overall, but my goal is to bring the readers up to speed about your history and connection to the culture.

You were born in Antigua, West Indies but grew up in Harlem while attending school in the Bronx. I was surprised to learn that your name didn't come from being a Deejay, but it came from you being a defensive warrior on the basketball court. Your friends called you "Red Alert" because of your natural reddish hair and your alertness on the defensive end of the basketball court. You graduated from DeWitt Clinton High School in the Bronx and was a top recruit to play college ball on a full athletic scholarship at Hampton University in Virginia. But after only three semesters at Hampton, you decided to come back home and follow your passion to become a fulltime Deejay for Afrika Bambaataa and the Universal Zulu Nation because of the influences of the Deejays you studied from, and one of those Deejays was DJ Kool Herc.

I think it is amazingly dope that your biological family tree runs deep within the roots of Hip-Hop culture. You got connected to Bambaataa through your cousin, the legendary DJ Jazzy Jay who moved to the Bronx River projects from Harlem. I can only imagine that seeing you and Jazzy Jay doing what you all were doing as Deejays sparked your nephew Mike G of the Jungle Brothers to take the path that he took in becoming an emcee. Not to mention your mother's house became the in-home studio and rendezvous for many Hip-Hop artists to create and hang out. It's almost like Hip-Hop was a part of your family's DNA because your fingerprints are all over Hip-Hop, from your involvement with the Universal Zulu Nation to the origins of the Violators with Chris Lighty to the organic formation of Native Tongues. I would have to agree with DJ EFN when he said, "There is a lineage and a legacy and an influence on artists like Kanye, Pharrell, Kendrick and so many other artists today that have been influenced directly and indirectly by what Native Tongues was doing."

This reminds me of one of my favorite movies, *It's A Wonderful Life,* where George Bailey discovers what life would be like if he didn't exist. Which makes me think: what would Hip-Hop be if you decided not to become a Deejay and instead stayed at Hampton University to hoop? Would Native Tongues have formed the way it did? Would Kanye, Pharrell, Kendrick and other artists who have been influenced directly and indirectly by Native Tongues exist today? Hip-Hop history would not be the same without you, Uncle Red.

You are celebrating 45 or 46 years as a Deejay, and you've been a Deejay on the radio for 38 years. You started Deejaying on the streets of NYC and then you started Deejaying on WRKS 98.7 KISS FM from 1982-94. From KISS you went to Hot 97 where you had two daily time slots from 1994-2001 (The Twelve O'Clock Old School at Noon Mix and The Five O'Clock Free Ride). From Hot 97 you went back to KISS-FM from 2001-2002. From there you started spinning for Power 105.1 FM for five years before going back to KISS-FM.

You were the Deejay with the signature *Yeaaaaaaaaaaaah*, and you pioneered the promo where you asked artists like Jungle Brothers w/Q-Tip, D-Nice, DJ Premier, and Fat Joe to create a promo song for you to play at the beginning of your radio shows on KISS FM. These promos actually became songs on albums, and it was an amazing way to bring people into the world of the Propmaster Wiz Kool DJ Red Alert.

I loved the conversation you had on Drink Champs regarding payola (the illegal practice of paying a commercial radio station Deejay to play a song. The number of times the songs are played can influence the perceived popularity of a song, and payola may be used to influence these meters), and your response showed me that you are a man of character and integrity. You said, "when you are being paid you are being owned." You take it as an insult for someone to give you money to play their music on the air. I love how you said that you would rather play a song that you believe in versus getting paid because taking money discredits your credibility as a Deejay.

You are the first NYC Deejay to do a lot of things:

- the first Deejay to work at all 4 NYC urban radio stations
- the first Deejay to record mix compilation albums
- the first Deejay to introduce dance hall music to mainstream radio
- the first Deejay to break the "Roxanne Roxanne" record by UTFO
- the first Deejay to break the "South Bronx" record by Boogie Down Productions
- the first to break in
  - the Jungle Brothers (through your nephew Mike G)
  - A Tribe Called Quest
  - Queen Latifah (through a relationship with DJ Mark the 45 King)
  - Black Sheep

You were a key figure in the introduction of Boogie Down Productions (DJ Scott La Rock (RIP) and KRS-One) during the legendary Bridge Wars. It can be said that you were a part of one of the very first Versuz: Boogie Down Productions and You versus Mr. Magic, Marley Marl, and MC Shan. Mr. Magic and Marley Marl swung first, breaking MC Shan's song "The Bridge" while you countered by breaking Boogie Down Productions song "South Bronx." Then the Juice Crew came back with a left-right combo with "Kill that Noise" while Boogie Down Productions switched to southpaw and came with the knockout blow, "The Bridge is Over" which pretty much *killed that noise* while you and the Boogie Down Productions crew ascended to new heights. You toured with Boogie Down Productions to be the "Spliff Star" to KRS-One as D-Nice was the Deejay. From hype man on tours, you went on to create Red Alert Productions to help the Jungle Brothers and A Tribe Called Quest go where they needed to. Your production company was the blueprint for Chris Lighty's Violator Management run.

You also talked about the importance of artists *paying dues* or homage to the artists who came before. I thought it was interesting when NORE talked about how the rappers of today don't seem to know about the Hip-Hop artists who came before them, and he asked the question of when did rap become dumb. You responded:

> The online/internet/social media world controls the minds of today because they are not thinking for themselves but thinking according to the perception of what they see and what they hear so they are not willing to go dig a little deeper [into the historical canon of Hip-Hop]. Paying dues has never stopped [and] the artists of today are cutting class and they need to go back to school.

I think the work that Drink Champs and the Boom Bap Chat are doing is important in the preservation of Hip-Hop history. Young people need to know the history and historical context of Hip-Hop.

There are not enough words in this letter to describe how much you have done for the advancement of the culture that I love so much. You are much more than a Deejay, Uncle Red, you are a Hip-Hop historian, an entrepreneur, a mentor, a teacher, an A&R, and now you are helping your son Kool G Mims, who is an emcee/rapper, take his career to levels of greatness. Again, you have done so much for the culture of Hip-Hop, and I would say that one of your greatest accomplishments is helping to create one of the greatest Hip-Hop crews ever assembled in the history of Hip-Hop culture - The Native Tongues.

To this I say thank you, much respect, and may the Most High continue to give you the strength to do what you do best: rock and spin on the one's and two's until you can't rock and spin any more.

From me and the Boom Bap Review Crew
peace & solidarity
iomos

CHAPTER THIRTY-TWO

The First Ladies of The Native Tongues

Written by iomos marad

I break into a lyrical freestyle
Grab the mic, look into the crowd and see smiles
Cause they see a woman standing up on her own two
Sloppy slouching is something I won't do
Some think that we can't flow (can't flow)
Stereotypes, they got to go (got to go)
I'mma mess around and flip the scene into reverse
(With what?) With a little touch of "Ladies First"

—Queen Latifah

Usually when people talk about the strength of Black women... they ignore the reality that to be strong in the face of oppression is not the same as overcoming oppression, that endurance is not to be confused with transformation

—bell hooks

The false narrative and perception of Hip-Hop and the game of rap music is that it has always been a male-dominated culture or genre of music. This statement might be true from a surface-level perspective, but when you dig a bit deeper into the historical context of Hip-Hop history, you will begin to realize the impact women (specifically Black women) have had on the culture of Hip-Hop overall. To be clear, women have always been present in the creation, movement, and transformation of Hip-Hop culture, but they often get erased as being placemakers and trailblazers—which is to be expected in a hyper-male-dominated world where this type of erasure is not surprising.

The humble beginnings of Hip-Hop culture began with the decision of one Jamaican woman by the name of Nettie Campbell who had enough courage to migrate to the United States. For those who may not know, Nettie Campbell is the mother of Clive Campbell aka DJ Kool Herc who many consider the father of Hip-Hop. In his book *Can't Stop Won't Stop*—Jeff Chang captures Nettie Campbell's decision to move to the United States:

> Nettie decided to supplement the family income by working and studying in the United States. Many other Jamaicans were already leaving for Miami, London, Toronto and New York City to escape the instability and seek their fortune...During the early 1960s, Nettie had departed from Manhattan to work as a dental technician and to study for a nursing degree. She saved money to send home and returned [to Jamaica] with a degree, convinced that the United States offered a better future for the family (Chang, 2005, p. 71).

Mama Campbell decided to move to the United States and her son Clive (the oldest of six children) was next to take the pilgrimage to join his mother in discovering this new world. After some years of making the sacrifice to live separately for the ultimate good of the family,[6] Cindy Campbell, Clive's sister, and

---

[6] Making sacrificial decisions to live apart for some time for the ultimate good of the family is the case for many immigrants.

the rest of the family moved to New York City and settled in the Bronx.

Next to Nettie, Cindy should be revered as another trailblazer and placemaker to the culture of Hip-Hop also because (believe it or not) it was her decision to throw the historical party on August 11, 1973 (the birth date of Hip-Hop) in the rec room of 1520 Sedgwick Avenue in the West Bronx that gave birth to the culture that we all love and celebrate today.

MC Pebblee Poo and MC Sha-Rock are two more female placemakers and trailblazers who should not be forgotten. Their contribution and legacy to Hip-Hop culture gets forgotten often, and their names are rarely mentioned. MC Pebblee Poo is known as the *very first emcee* to rock the mic at the legendary DJ Kool Herc Bronx parties as the elements of Hip-Hop began to form. MC Sha-Rock (also known as the mother of the Mic) is noted as the first female emcee-rapper of Hip-Hop culture *on wax* or to be recorded on vinyl from Hip-Hop's inception in the 1970s. On February 14, 1981 (Valentine's Day), Sha-Rock became the first female emcee to appear on the national television show Saturday Night Live as a member of the Funky 4+1.[7] The contributions and legacies of these amazing Black women should never be forgotten, and I hope this small article is playing its part in celebrating and remembering what they all brought to the creation and formation of Hip-Hop culture.

I write for those women who do not speak, for those who do not have a voice because they are so terrified, because we are taught to respect fear more than

---

[7] MC Sha-Rock is the +1 more in the Funky 4+1.

ourselves. We have been taught that silence would save us, but it won't.

—Audre Lorde

The ladies will kick it the rhyme that is wicked
Those that don't know how to be pros get evicted
A woman can bear you break you take you
Now it's time to rhyme can you relate to
A sister dope enough to make you holler and scream
— (Queen Latifah off "Ladies First" from *All Hail the Queen,* 1989)

It is important to mention Nettie and Cindy Campbell, MC Pebblee Poo, and MC Sha-Rock because I believe the women I am about to mention as *The First Ladies of The Native Tongues* stand on the shoulders of the aforementioned placemakers and trailblazers of Hip-Hop. The first ladies of The Native Tongues are Queen Latifah, Monie Love, Shortie No Mass, and Vinia Mojica.

In 1989, the world was introduced to Dana Owens aka Queen Latifah (hailing from Newark & East Orange, New Jersey) through her first album *All Hail the Queen* followed by *Nature of a Sista, Black Reign, Order in the Court* and three more albums to follow. She found her emcee name Latifah in a book of Arabic names which means *delicate* and *very kind* when she was just eight years old. The name Latifah might mean delicate and very kind, but her approach to emceeing is quite the opposite. I believe her love for reading intricate books like this was instilled in her by her mother Rita Limae who was a schoolteacher at her alma mater Irvington High School in New Jersey. Whenever I hear Latifah breathe life into the mic, I hear the knowledge and confidence of Angela Davis, Assata Shakur and Bessie Smith, also known as the "Empress of the Blues." This would explain why Latifah is known as *The Queen of Rap.*

My introduction to Queen Latifah was from her monumental video "Ladies First" featuring Monie Love from her *All Hail the Queen* album. All I can say is I lost it the first time I saw this video. Being raised by a single Black woman on the South Side of Chicago, I instinctively knew that women (specifically Black women) were first in my community and meant so much to the world, but they were often overlooked and not given the proper respect they were due. "Ladies First" echoed the sentiments of Audre Lorde when she wrote that she writes for women who do not speak or have a voice because they are too afraid. Well, Queen Latifah took up Lorde's mantle and also showed that she had the courage to speak for women who could not speak through the microphone or given space to speak in any form for that matter. I thought it was amazing to see two Super *SHE*-roes on *Yo! MTV Raps*, breathing fearlessly complicated intellectual back-and-forth rhymes about what it meant to them to be Black women accompanied by flashing images of legendary Black women of the past who are as much a part of American and World history as any other women. As I was watching the video, it made me instantly think about my mother and my grandmother, and it gave me the vision of the type of Black woman I knew I wanted to marry, which I did. Latifah continued to be the voice of voiceless women with her Grammy award-winning song "U.N.I.T.Y." which spoke to the misogyny in our society, domestic violence, and the need for peace.[8] Latifah was introduced to Red Alert through DJ Mark the 45 King, and that was Latifah's introduction to becoming a member of The Native Tongues. Latifah went on to appear and star on television shows like *The Fresh Prince of Bel Air*, *Hangin' with Mr. Cooper*, and of course *Living Single*.[9] From

---

[8] From Tayanna Lee McQuillar's phenomenal book *When Rap Music Had a Conscience: The Artists, Organizations, and Historic Events that Inspired and Influenced the Golden Age of Hip-Hop from 1987 to 1996* with foreword by Brother J of X-Clan.

television, she went on to appear and star in movies such as *Set It Off*, *Just Wright* (starring Common), and *Brown Sugar*. Queen Latifah has won too many awards to mention for her role in the film community and her contribution to Hip-Hop culture as the original First Lady of The Native Tongues.

Yo, praise me not for simply being what I am
Born in L-O-N-D-O-N and sound American
You dig exactly where I'm coming from
You want righteous rhyming, I'mma give you some
To enable you to aid yourself and get paid
And the material that has no meaning I wish to slay
Pay me every bit of your attention
Like mother, like daughter, I would also like to mention

I wish for you to bring me to, bring me to the rhythm
Of which is now systematically given
Desperately stressing I'm the daughter of a sister
Who's the mother of a brother who's the brother of another
Plus one more; all four
Have a job to do, we doing it
Respect due, to the mother who's the root of it
And next up is me, the M-O-N-I-E L-O-V-E
And I'm first cause I'm a L-A-D-I-E
   (Monie Love from "Ladies First" off *All Hail the Queen*,
                                                          1989)

---

[9] The television show *Friends* was based on *Living Single* which did not get the recognition and love that *Friends* did possibly because of the complexion of the cast.

Simone Antionette Johnson, better known as Monie Love—who I consider one of the greatest British emcees of all time along with Slick Rick—was introduced to my eyes and ears through Queen Latifah's "Ladies First" video, like I mentioned above. After appearing on "Ladies First," Monie Love dropped her solo album *Down To Earth*, featuring the standout songs "Monie In the Middle", "It's a Shame (My Sister)", and "Swiney Swiney." "Monie in the Middle" was nominated for Best Rap Solo performance only to end up second behind MC Hammer's "Can't Touch This." Monie released a second album entitled *In a Word or 2* and went on to work with LA Reid & Babyface, Whitney Houston, and Prince. Prince produced a song on Monie Love's second album entitled "Born to B.R.E.E.D (Build Relationships where Education and Enlightenment Dominate)." This brilliant acronym pushes back on the idea or belief that the purpose of women is to only give birth to children—which we all know they do so much more. Monie Love's introduction to The Native Tongues came by way of her meeting the Jungle Brothers when they were in London. Monie and Afrika of the Jungle Brothers were in a relationship. Monie moved to the States and the rest is Hip-Hop history.

Terressa Thompson, better known as Shortie No Mass (*I am Shortie. I be 4-11*) was born in Boston, Massachusetts, and relocated to Philadelphia, Pennsylvania as a child. According to Shortie No Mass' website, she has always been a creative soul with a passion for writing. Over the years, she has been hailed as one of the best female MCs.[10] Shortie No Mass caught the world's attention in 1993 when she was featured on De La Soul's third album *Buhloone Mindstate*, where her presence and energy

---

[10] shortienomass.com

was felt throughout.[11] From Shortie asking Dres, *who you here with?* on the song "En Focus" or her telling Dave *you be buggin'* while giving a memorable ad lib to Pos' saying *man, I'd rather put a pistol atcha head and try to burst iiiiiiiiiiiiiiiiiit* while breathing fire on her rhyme to let the people know who and what Shortie No Mass was all about on the song "In the Woods":

Can I come off with the rest of em I think I should
Could I? Of course, one verse now ya lost it
Found it realizing I came off it sounds mean
But pal, there's a new kid on the scene
I got much soul on the down-low tip
Lay back smooth, one drink I'll be trippin

Never don't you dare consider me a fly gal
Pal, I got props on a different tip
I recall back I go for mine, I get the goods
Wouldn't you know, forgot my compass, I got lost in the woods
Found my way and I was out I pronounce every letter
And if I had the chance I'd do it better
I heard a holler down the way and now I'm out for the time being
Ya wanna be in but you can't see what I'm seein'
Time and time, my friend, I stay gettin it on
And now they playin my song again

(Shortie No Mass from "In the Woods" by De La Soul off *Buhloone Mindstate*, 1993)

During Boom Bap Chat interview number 98, Shortie shared with us that she was traveling back and forth from Philly to New York during the recording of *Buhloone Mindstate* when she was finishing up high school. She had to tell her school counselor to

---

[11] Shortie No Mass also featured on the Roots debut album *Organix* in the same year

just give her all of her schoolwork to complete so she could graduate while she was recording and about to go on tour. After the release of *Buhloone Mindstate*, Shortie toured America with De La, Tribe Called Quest, Tha Alkaholics, and Souls of Mischief. She also performed with The Roots in London.

Since becoming a peripheral member of The Native Tongues by way of her *big brother* relationship with Posdnous of De La, she has had the pleasure of working with historic artists such as Grandmaster Flash, The Roots, Scott Storch, Da Beatminerz, Rockwilder, The Dogg Pound's Kurupt, DJ Jazzy Jeff, Monie Love, Kid Sister and Kanye West. Shortie just released her newest album *Here Goes Nothing* (with production by Da Beatminerz, J-Zone, and her son Jay Law) on December 16, 2021, to fulfill a request from the late great Phife Dawg heard on the intro of the album. And since her resurgence in 2021, she has more music in store for the listeners of the world to enjoy to keep The Native Tongues legacy alive.

The thing that men and women need to do is stick together
Progressions can't be made if we're separate forever
I hooked this funky beat with the loop and the feature
With the funky singing by Miss Vinia Mojica
(Q-Tip from "Verses from the Abstract" off *The Low End Theory* by A Tribe Called Quest, 1991)

Last and definitely not the least is Miss Vinia A. Mojica, hailing from Queens, NYC. Vinia is a singer and songwriter, and she has been featured on so many songs with The Native Tongues and other peripheral members that I consider her to be one of the Ladies of Native Tongues. Vinia's introduction to the world and into the Native Tongue family came by way of being featured on the Jungle Brothers' "Acknowledge Your Own History" song on their second album *Done By the Forces of Nature* in 1989. Vinia beautifully sang the meaning of the colors for the Pan-African flag created by Marcus Garvey.

The Red's for the blood
And the Black's for the man
The Green is the color that stands for the land

From there, Vinia's singing services were requested by the rest of The Native Tongues members and other iconic Hip-Hop groups. Miss Mojica's voice can be heard on the following Hip-Hop artist's songs:

- A Tribe Called Quest, "Verses from the Abstract", *The Low End Theory* (1991)
- De La Soul, "A Roller Skating Jam Named 'Saturdays'", *De La Soul is Dead* (1991)
- Pete Rock & CL Smooth, "Searching", *The Main Ingredient* (1994)
- Heavy D, "Nothing but Love", *Nothing but Love* (1995)
- Heltah Skeltah, "Therapy", *Nocturnal* (1996)
- Heavy D, "Waterbed Hev", *Waterbed Hev* (1997)
- Pete Rock, "Mind Blowin", *Soul Survivor* (1998)
- Black Star, "K.O.S. (Determination)", *Mos Def & Talib Kweli Are Black Star* (1998)
- Mos Def, "Climb", *Black on Both Sides* (1999)
- Alliance Ethnik, "Honesty & Jalousie", *Honesty et Jalousie (fais un choix dans la vie)* (1995)
- "Respect", "Fat Come Back", "Tu Sais Quoi", and "5 Heures Du Mat" from *Fat Comeback* (1999)
- Reflection Eternal, "The Blast", *Train of Thought* (2000)
- Da Beatminerz, "Take That", *Brace 4 Impak* (2001)

- Hi-Tek, "The Sun God" and "Get Ta Steppin", *Hi-Teknology* (2001)
- Talib Kweli, "Stand to the Side", *Quality* (2002)
- DJ Mehdi, "Anything Is Possible", *(The Story of) Espion* (2002)
- Common, "Ferris Wheel", *Electric Circus* (2002)
- DJ Spinna, "Idols", *Here to There* (2003)

In the article *An Ode to Vinia Mojica Because Today is a Good Day for Flowers*, Panama Jackson wrote:

> Her voice is so soulful it's no wonder she was so in-demand from the Native Tongues crew and the surrounding crews. Her voice: it's like butter, baby; it's like sugar, y'all. It's versatile enough to be used in myriad ways. For instance, on the insanely beautiful record "The Sun God," by Common on Hi-Tek's debut Hi-Teknology, her voice is used as an instrument but it's so necessary and adds so much in the way of painting an aural picture, which is saying something, especially because the beat already tells its own story. Which was fairly common for her on so many of the songs I know and love (Jackson, 2021).

All I can say to Panama's words is, I concur. Miss Mojica's voice is so pure and angelic yet alien to anything you have ever heard before at the same time. And even though her vocals are often in the background of songs, if you took her vocals off of those songs, you would instantly feel the absence of her voice. I wanted Miss Mojica to release a solo album so badly. *Fortunately*, I own the 12-inch she released in 2003 with the songs *Guilt Junky* on the A-Side and *Sands of Time* on the B-Side but *unfortunately* she never released a full-length album. Do you ever feel like there is something missing in the world? Well, for me, a full-length project from Miss Vinia Mojica is missing from this world, and I think the world would be a much better place to cohabitate in if it had more of Miss Vinia Mojica's voice in it.

I would like to end with this:

Dear Miss Vinia Mojica,

I would like to thank you for everything you have given to us as listeners and lovers of Hip-Hop. All those songs you are featured on above would not be what they are without your voice and presence. The Native Tongues and Hip-Hop culture as a whole would not be what it is today without the gift of your voice that you unselfishly shared with us all. I don't know where you are or if you are still singing, but I hope and pray you are because your beautiful voice is a blessing to the world. Just like the toast Dre made to Sidney in the movie *Brown Sugar*, "you are the perfect voice over a tight beat."

In peace & solidarity,
iomos of the Boom Bap Chat crew.

Part Four
Live Interviews

CHAPTER THIRTY-THREE
Live Interview with Mike G of Jungle Brothers

As conducted by iomos marad

In February 2019, before COVID-19 was considered a pandemic, my wife purchased tickets for us to see the Jungle Brothers and KRS-One with J. Rawls as the host/DJ of the event in Akron, Ohio for my birthday. I had two missions in my mind. Mission 1: Get my *Youth Culture Power* book signed by J. Rawls (completed). Mission 2: Purchase a KRS-One or Jungle Brothers T-Shirt, or both. I didn't see any KRS-One merch for sale, but I did see that The Jungle Brothers were selling T-shirts. As I was buying some J-Beez T-shirts, I asked Mike G if he remembered hanging out with Tone B. Nimble and some members of the Family Tree at a studio in Chicago working on some songs. He was like, "Yeah, I remember that." I told him a funny story of why I wasn't able to make the studio session that day, and we both laughed. Long story short, we exchanged numbers with the intention for me to reconnect Mike G with Tone B. Nimble, and it's crazy how divine connections and meetings happen for other reasons. Fast forward a few years, and we decided to write a book dedicated to The Native Tongues. Getting Mike G's number that night is the reason the interview you are about to read exists.

iomos: Right before the pandemic, I saw you and the Jungle Brothers perform live in Akron, OH. KRS-One performed that night as well. It was an amazing show. It was Hip-Hop through and through. I wanted to ask you, first and foremost, what influenced you to get into Hip-Hop?

Mike G: My influences came early. I grew up under Red Alert. So, aside from the regular street stuff, I was front row watching Crazy Legs battle kids from my junior high school back in the days and graffiti. Straight up, I used to bomb a little bit. Red bringing home the tape from Bronx River and Harlem World and all these other spots, T connection - I was in from there. So, it has been a long while.

iomos: So, you said you used to bomb and do graffiti. Was that your first intro into Hip-Hop before you started emceeing?

Mike G: Yeah, I would say that. Because during that time period, Red would bring the tapes and I would write here and there. But when I got to high school was when I really came out of my shell. But even during the summer leading up to high school is when I met Sammy and we would go around the block parties and I would get on. That was my real first step right before high school.

iomos: Speaking of high school, Murry Bergtraum High School is legendary. It's a business school known for marketing, finance, human resources, and things like that. But it's also known for producing Hip-Hop's greatest icons like yourself, Afrika, Ali Shaheed Muhammad, Q-Tip, and Brother J from X

	Clan. I am probably missing some brothers. But what was that like?
Mike G:	It was dope. I lived in Harlem and Queens, but I spent most of my time growing up in Harlem. And then I went to junior high school in the Bronx. My junior high was wild, it was straight wild. And it was wilder than my high school. And it was still that Hip-Hop influence there. But when I got to high school, they had more talent shows and other shows. I can't remember what they were called. But the performance of Hip-Hop came out more. Junior high school was more raw. Cats would be at the arcade right outside the school, the center, cats would be B-boying, emceeing sometimes, but mostly electro boogie and breakdancing. So, it was a great time.
iomos:	Because your middle school was so wild, is that why you chose to go to Murry Bergtraum?
Mike G:	No, to be honest. There was another school, John F. Kennedy. They were known for sports, and it would be my next step. But my pops was like, "No, we got to get you on something more stable." So, he's like, "Let's get you down in the city." That's how I wound up going to Murry Bergtraum. I had to pick a couple of other schools. Murry Bergtraum accepted me and there it is.
iomos:	Is that where you met Afrika?
Mike G:	Yeah.

iomos: How did the Jungle Brothers form? How did you guys come together as a group?

Mike G: I think my first year (at Murry Bergtraum), there was a variety show – that is what it was called. They were putting together a variety show and a couple of cats got together. I think cats were just trying to figure out who was going to rock with who. There were a couple of us - it was me, Af(rika), Pop, Shawn Do, another dude, the colonel and another guy- and we were all just kind of spitting. Me and Af kind of clicked. So, it was me, him, a guy named Brooklyn B, oh and Brother J. So, it's me, Brother J, Brooklyn B, and Af.

I tell the story all the time now. Brother J was an amazing beatboxer, and his tone was off the chain. He was a monster with it. And then Brooklyn B was the original DJ. That just didn't work out. There was a little friction, I guess. So, Sammy came in his spot because I had been rocking with Sammy. I knew Sammy through my uncle. Then Brother J wanted to do his own thing and just killed them on the beatbox. So, the pieces fell away and it just wound up being me, Afrika, and Sammy.

iomos: How crazy would that have been if it was you, Afrika, and Brother J in the Jungle Brothers?! Let me tell you this, straight up, I'm from the south side of Chicago. There was a time I had no idea what I wanted to do with my life. I had an older cousin named Leon Rogers. He used to go to this secret spot to get Hip-Hop cassettes. He went on his little journey one time and then he called me like, "Bro, you need to come up here right now." I went around the corner and my cousin had his window's open, the front door open, the screen door open, and he was bumping *Straight out the Jungle*. And as I'm walking to the house, I'm hearing, "Educated man from the motherland..." and I'm like, "Who is this?" When I came in, he gave me the cassette tape. I looked at that cassette tape for hours while I listened to it. That album changed my life.

Mike G: Wow, thank you.

iomos: When I heard Afrika say that ("Educated man from the motherland"), I was like, "Yeah, that's what I want to be. I want to be an educated black man" and that's how I got into education.

Mike G: That's deep. That's deep.

iomos: *Straight out the Jungle* is a very monumental album to Hip-Hop culture. What does that album mean to you?

Mike G: *Straight out the Jungle* in a way was my ode to Hip-Hop because leading up to it, that was when I graduated high school. Prior to that, it's like I had lived a lifetime, and I was only like 18, 19. I just wanted to get to a point where people could take something away from it because that's what I got from watching the pioneers - the Grandmaster Cazes, the Cold Crushes, the Furious Fives, the Spoonie Gs. Those were the people I really came up on. Those are my top fives, my heroes.

I guess the same way that you felt when you heard *Straight out the Jungle* is the same way I felt when I heard Cold Crush routines or the Fantastic Five - when Cold Crush was like, "You know it's us, the Cold Crush!" So, just wanting to bring that type of enjoyment, excitement, and love and honesty. Just everyday, I wanted to paint that picture - straight out the jungle. It was like New York was a crazy time, but it was also great. It was crazy, it was majestic, so we tried to portray that in the music.

Afrika would lay down a lot of tones. We would go back and forth. He would pick a lot of samples and he would play things, and we'd be like "nah, this, not that," but he definitely spearheaded a lot of the tracks between him, Sammy, Red - just that vibe - it all poured into *Straight out the Jungle.*

iomos: That album doesn't get the props that it deserves.

Mike G: It was in the 80s. It wasn't well documented for what it's worth, but it was a great time.

iomos: That's why we are working on this book: to celebrate you all because y'all influenced a lot of lives. Going back to that concert I mentioned earlier with you all and KRS-One. KRS was talking about how the music changed people's lives. The music you made and KRS and Poor Righteous Teachers and X-Clan—just that era in general—inspired people to be doctors, lawyers, community workers, social workers, just because of the music you all created. So we definitely want to give you flowers through this book. That's why we are working on this book.

Mike G: Thanks man. That's solid.

iomos: After *Straight out the Jungle,* y'all did *Done by the Forces of Nature.* It was another great album. What was the idea behind creating that body of work, to create that album?

Mike G: Thank you. That also came from experience because we got to travel. We did a lot of dates around New York and up and down the East Coast a bit. But our first major tour - we were on a plane going to Europe and we got to spend months out there, a month and a half or so. We took that, and we saw how different people really rocked to us, how different countries were creating their own Hip-Hop scenes (with) different languages, but we come over speaking English, they know all the records word for word, then coming back here seeing the same type of love, seeing that common thread throughout the world with music. And at that time, there definitely wasn't any internet, there was no social media. It was all about phone calls and Video Music Box popping up. We were in London, I remember they only had two channels. This was in England! You only had two channels, and the TV cut off at 11 o'clock or some craziness. And going to Germany at the time, the wall was still up. Skinheads were out there running around crazy. Then you come home, you got skinheads over here and you still have ballbusters - it was crazy.

For me, it was definitely the travel, being able to see the world and then really soak in the experience from *Straight out the Jungle,* getting to travel, hearing all different new sounds and coming back, and I just wanted to open up as much as possible and show people that life, just speak my experience.

iomos: You could tell the difference in production, too, from *Straight out the Jungle* to *Done by the Forces of Nature*. *Done by the Forces of Natures* sounds more mature.

Mike G: Oh yeah. Definitely. We literally recorded *Straight out the Jungle* like on 8-track. By the time we got to *Done by the Forces of Nature,* we had locked down a deal with Warner Brothers, got a bigger budget, bigger studio, and more tools to create with. So that definitely showed. (We had) more time, more thought got to go into it. We had time doing *Straight out the Jungle,* but we were writing rhymes on a train going to the studio and after homework. So by the time we got to *Done by the Forces of Nature*, we had like all day, weeks upon weeks and just a lot of time and a lot more experience and a lot more money for that matter, which got us into Calliope which was one of the top studios at the time.

iomos: Okay Player released an article a year ago about a project you all had called *Crazy Wisdom Masters.* Can you speak on how that project came about and what happened? Can we hear it somewhere?

Mike G: Oh, yeah, it's out and about. You could Google it, you can Google just about anything nowadays. We did such a run on *Done by the Forces of Nature*, and we just went in for the most part. To be 100%, we were smoking mad weed, we were out all the time, traveling crazy, really getting a mix of how to run the circuit, like running tours and stuff like that. And we were zero to 60 every day. So, it was like a lot of that came out, wanting to stretch the sound. That was really what it was about, not being afraid to step out in a box of what contemporary Hip-Hop was at that time, and really manipulating the drum patterns. We had that on there and just having fun, to be honest, had a lot of fun. And we worked with some great guys, introduction to Bootsy, and Mudbone and Bill Laswell, George Clinton, all these guys, Parliament, that was a heavy time for us.

And then just a big miscommunication, I think, because being on Warner Brothers, they just want you to really constantly click on what's popular like the dance stuff, "What U Waitin' 4" (and) "I'll House You" and stuff like that. So, we were on to the next, it's that style of sampling. You only really heard necks once Wu-Tang started jumping out, but we were already doing that. But they (Warner Brothers) didn't see it. So, just turn the corner. Now it's the legend of the Crazy Wisdom Masters. But that style of production, we were already doing it.

iomos: That's crazy how labels don't see or accept the progression of artists. It's always this conflict between labels and artists' vision and where they are trying to go artistically. Being signed onto a label brings barriers and speed bumps to the progression.

Mike G: Yeah, because you need a constant translator. When you get the Warner Brothers type of people, that type of atmosphere, and they are not really traveling back and forth to the studio keeping in touch with a particular artist, and it gets lost in translation. Even with the audience, you have to constantly show growth. The story has to be constantly in people's faces so they can keep up.

iomos: So now let's talk a little bit about The Native Tongues. What did Native Tongues mean to you? And what does it mean to you now?

Mike G: That was my first big Hip-Hop posse. So, being at that level in music and then having that camaraderie with all those other groups, that felt good because you ultimately have the respect of your peers and stuff like that. And that felt real solid. And just that brotherhood and family vibe when it came to the music, that probably meant the most to me. That's what I liked and enjoyed the most. And then the way people enjoyed it and always wanted to see it - it was like a continuous birthday party - every day is your birthday.

iomos: I tell people all the time that there are only two crews in life I want to be a part of - Native Tongues and Boot Camp Clik. You guys were great. Native Tongues was it for me. It was just an amazing movement. I love the connection between the Zulu Nation, too, and what the Zulu Nation stood for. I felt like it was this synergy between Native Tongues and Zulu Nation.

Mike G: Yeah, that's what I came up under. In essence they pioneered the New York Hip-Hop sound, Zulu Nation. So, that's what it was.

iomos: Me and my crew have been asking people all the time, "Who are the core members of The Native Tongues?" It always depends on who you ask. So, my crew was like, "Be sure to ask Mike G that!" Ask him, "Who would you say are the core members of The Native Tongues?"

Mike G: Oh, of course, definitely myself, Bam, Sammy, Mase, Pos, Dave, Ali, Tip, Phife, Jarobi, Monie, Latifah, Dres, and Lawnge pulling in the rear. And Chi-Ali straggling along. And that's not to hate on none of the other artists that came after him, like the Black Stars or whatever else you want to add to the mix. But for me, that's the official call - was the first three groups, along with Monie and Latifah because we were all really out there like that. And then even Chi for that matter was there early. And Lawnge came up. Red met Lawnge on the road when he was touring with KRS. Lawnge came up to New York and hung with us (and) stayed with us.

iomos: So, who would you say are the affiliates... or you don't just...

Mike G: I don't even get into that. Whoever it is and that is not to hate. They'll say Leaders of the New School, Brand Nubian. All the groups that really embrace that time period.

iomos: I know Red Alert is your uncle. It was so dope seeing him on Drink Champs. I watched that

	episode like two or three times. I love the knowledge that he has on Hip-Hop. What do you think Red Alert means to Hip-Hop culture? And what do you think he meant to The Native Tongues?
Mike G:	To the culture, now he's like a time capsule, like a precious stone. It's like I said he was the witness because early on, the only things we had were cassette tapes and Video Music Box. And before that, it was really just cassette tapes. So, to have somebody who is certified, was there (and) pretty much watched the transition from the DJ booth (and) watching all the records come along, the whole gamut. He's like a history teacher; he is like a historian. A DJ's job is to give people what they want, in a sense, but they also still try to keep their own identity by pumping what they vibe into it and spreading their vibe. He is one. Kid Capri is one. So many other DJs, but to be able to come from that time period all the way up 'til now, constantly staying in the forefront through radio and playing out... priceless.
iomos:	Yeah, I agree 100%. What gap would there be in Hip-Hop and just in American culture in general if Jungle Brothers didn't exist?
Mike G:	I don't know that one. Not sure I could answer that. Maybe I'm too modest to answer, but I think that eventually that vibe would have come out because Hip-Hop early on was always different, unlike today where a lot of the theme is the same all across the board. The differences and all the different

artists, The Poor Righteous Teachers, Fresh Prince and Steady B, Just-Ice, the difference was there. Joeski Love, Slick Rick, just the difference between each artist, the characters, our theme, our shine, our swag, everybody had such original swag all to their own in that time period.

iomos: Yeah, that's amazing. We interviewed Shortie No Mass, and she was talking about when she got with De La Soul to work on *Buhloone Mindstate*, that The Native Tongues had disbanded. She said it was kind of like they didn't really speak on it that much. Can you speak about what you think happened to The Native Tongues movement? If you don't feel comfortable answering that question, that's cool.

Mike G: It was like everybody grew up. It got political not just with people's lives, but also being on the different majors. The majors had a part to play because they each wanted to take advantage of (the groups). You had three popping groups in three different majors, not even majors, but just three different labels. And they all wanted to make the most for each of their artists. So, you have a lot of that going on and just growing.

iomos: Do you think a movement like The Native Tongues is needed today? I just feel like that movement that you all created - I think that needs to be duplicated today for young people to see.

Mike G: In a sense, it is, and one person who I got to definitely put on that pedestal is J. Cole. He comes across as clear and solid, his themes are broad, they're not one-sided, and he really has a good

	perspective for what's going on. I think it's out there. It's just a different generation, so it's hard; it's like we need a translator. But it won't get lost in translation. The vibe is definitely there. I think he constantly references Tribe. So he definitely drops the Tribe reference here and there.
iomos:	That leads me to my next question. What newer Hip-Hop artists besides J. Cole are you listening to today? And why, what do you see in them?
Mike G:	Oh, I couldn't tell you really, to be honest. I listen to a lot of old stuff. I listen to new stuff too. I listen to Rick Ross and Styles. I listen to a little bit of everything. And definitely Nipsey. Definitely we got a lot of joints. There's a lot of good Hip-Hop out right now. It's just a lot, that is the thing. You can't even keep up.
iomos:	I was wondering, do you all still stay connected? Any of you all from Native Tongues? Is it still like family, that bond? Are y'all still connected?
Mike G:	Oh, yeah, to a certain extent. I mean we still all rap. I just spoke to Pos and Mase not too long ago. Me and Dres playing phone tag. But we are all old, everybody got kids now, so it is a little different. But I think overall, the family vibe is still there. Folks ain't get together in a while.
iomos:	Another thing Shortie No Mass said was that a Native Tongue tour would be dope. Do you think that would ever happen? That would be so dope.
Mike G:	Yeah, that would be dope.

iomos: I will have to follow y'all from state to state. I'd have to tell my wife, "Look, I'll be gone for a couple of weeks. I'm just going to be following this tour."

Mike G: Yeah, I feel you. Never say never. I know a lot of the heads amongst us (are) always thinking about it. So, there is still a chance.

iomos: Are the Jungle Brothers working on anything new? Are any new projects coming out or anything?

Mike G: Well, we dropped an album right at the beginning of the pandemic. We got that up on our website, www.junglebrothers4life.com. We got a couple of vinyl projects coming out. Sam did a mixtape. He's working on Volume Two now (and) that'll also be up on the website. Afrika is doing a couple of different projects. You just kind of have to search for him. So yeah, definitely check us out there.

iomos: Do you have any solo stuff coming up?

Mike G: Nah. We'll see. It's always asked but never get through to it. But I've done a couple of tracks with Do Me, Cadence, and a couple of these dudes - YZ from back in the days, a part of Great Minds. Did that, so yeah, I stay productive.

iomos: That's all the questions that I have right now. Do you have any last words you want to say or anything?

Mike G: No, thanks for having me, man, I look forward to it. Hopefully, (we) will get out to Chi(cago) soon. I got

	a call from out there about a month ago, hopefully, we'll get out there.
iomos:	No doubt. Have a great evening. Thank you. Thank you for your time.
Mike G:	All right, man.
iomos:	Yes, sir. Salute.
Mike G:	Talk to you soon. Peace.
iomos:	Peace.

CHAPTER THIRTY-FOUR

Live Interview with Dres of Black Sheep

As conducted by MC Till, iomos marad, & Profound

This interview with Dres took place as part of the Boom Bap Chat podcast that originally aired on Thursday, June 2nd, 2022. Dres gave us so much to ponder that night. We did not transcribe the entire interview. That would have been darn near another book in length! We tried to edit the interview as best we could to extract most or at least a good amount of the stories and wisdom Dres dropped on us that night. To hear the full interview, simply find podcast #104 of the Boom Bap Chat wherever you like to stream your podcasts. Hope you enjoy the edited written version of that interview.

Till: Hey Dres, how are you?

Dres: I'm good. Just been really, really busy. I feel like I'm recuperating. Just finished dropping this Stu Bangas project, and it was very busy for me. We dropped 4 videos in 4 weeks. Stu is an amazing producer and has a long, long life in front of him in Hip-Hop. He is a beautiful cat as well.

Till: Let's jump into that album (*Sheep Stu*). Your debut came out over three decades ago, and your music today sounds like you just came out yesterday. You sound as fresh as ever, your wordplay is on point. You sound hungry. How do you keep that hunger and that top tier level all these years later?

Dres: It is a combination of things. I've always stayed busy. After the major label releases, I learned how to navigate on my own. I've been releasing independent projects on my own. I've always been there. I might not have been on everyone's radar. I've always been a student, and I've always been competitive. I'm proud to always be the Black Sheep, to go against the grain. Let me show you what is poppin' as opposed to tell you. I'd rather show you. That's kind of where the hunger comes from. Let me show you where I come from. It's like a wise man telling a rich man how to spend his money. A rich man will never adheed to a wise man's words if the wise is not rich. In this scenario with Hip-Hop being what it is - it's kind of a bloodsport. The young definitely try to eat the elders. It is not for me to tell a young cat how he can win as much as it is for me to show him. It's simple. All I do is do what I think is dope. I don't do what I think they think is dope. I do what I think is dope.

Till: That reminds of the last time we talked. You were giving props to the younger generation for having their business together and the way in which they are able to connect and use all these different platforms. It feels like you and Stu Bangas clicked and figured something out with this project. Can you speak to how you clicked and the philosophy of the rollout for the album?

Dres: That was done so intentionally. If you put out a full LP, literally the next week after you drop 15 songs, people are going to be like "so what else do you got?" To me, it borders disrespect - to do 15 songs that are top-notch and for people to look at it so whimsical. I wanted to take the time, and I didn't want to do a full album to get this point across. I wanted to do an EP. What happens if you do this? How many sales do you accumulate by creating a hard sale and dropping and pushing a single every week so that every week there is a blog talking about it and let's (also) put a visual to it. What happens if you do that every week and then release your project? People are investing themselves into what you are doing as opposed to you dropping 15 songs or even 5 songs. Cats skim through it and pick what they might like for their playlist and disregard the rest. That's kind of what I've seen music become. I wanted people to be a little more vested. I wanted to find out, can you create a hard sale in these days of streaming? Streaming for an artist like me is horrible. I wanted to create a hard sale and tempt people with music every week and make it available to them. We created a bundle so that if you like what you are hearing at any point of time, you can purchase a CD, a T-Shirt and a poster of this project that we are coming out of left field with but is really stellar. You can see the thought that was put into it. The mixing was done by my dude Peter Miser and mastered by Bob Power. This is a top tier project - something that every Hip-Hop head should own! It is one thing to like something. It is another thing to support something.

Till: Likes and hearts don't pay bills.

Dres: Not at all.

Till: Before we move on from the Sheep Stu project, I wanted to ask you one more question about it. This project has a little more of an edge to it as compared to your past music. Was that Stu Bangas bringing that out of you? Did you want to be more aggressive with this one?

Dres: Yeah, it was kind of intentional. When I was knee-deep in the D&D (Dilla and Dres) project, I met Stu because someone tagged me in a beat that Stu did on IG. I thought, *oh wow, this is hard*. It is one thing for something to be hard. It's another thing for something to be soulful as well. I felt like Stu had a nice combination of both. It invoked in me just a little bit more of being on the block. There was a little skip to what he was doing.

Till: Part of us writing this book is us saying thank you to the Native Tongues. It is also a celebration. You all set off a movement that set off something in us. Hopefully others will see something in us that will set something off in them and it will keep going.

Dres: That's dope. Word up.

Till: So tonight, we wanted to get your commentary on a few Native Tongues albums. I'll name an album and, if a story or commentary comes to mind, we would love to soak that up. First up is *People's Instinctive Travels and the Paths of Rhythm* by A Tribe Called Quest.

Dres: A very cool time in my life. During the making of that album is me bumping into Mista Lawnge. I'm just getting out of a bunch of trouble. I'm working, going to school, and got my first appointment. I bump into Mista Lawnge, and we lock in and he is going to come stay with me. I was just getting out of a bunch of trouble, and I wasn't trying to go back. I had to find myself a little bit, had to structure myself more than anything. I started to pal around with Mista Lawnge like, "What are you getting into?" He's like, "I'm going to the studio." I'm like, "Word? I'm going with you." I go to Calliope studios with Lawnge, and it might have been a Tribe session for *Peoples*. Lawnge didn't really tell me what I was walking into. He just brought me. Tip and them didn't have a record out then so there was no wow factor in meeting Tribe. At that moment, they were some guys I was meeting in the studio working on music. There was definitely a wow factor to meeting the Jungle Brothers and De La and Queen Latifah and Red Alert. I'm telling Lawnge, "Yo, you know these cats, like WHAT?!" Lawnge was real familiar with everyone. You could see he had been around cats for a minute. I was really proud of him. He and Tip are really cool. They always talked beats. Lawnge is literally responsible for a beat or two on that album (*People's Instinctive Travels and the Paths of Rhythm*). It might be the beat for "Can I Kick It." I'm not sure. I'd have to ask Lawnge. But they (Tip and Lawnge) were that cool. I'm taking it all in and I'm really impressed by everyone's ability. Cats are dope. Even then honing their own skills, they were willing to leave it all out there. Cats were freestyling non-stop. Cats were always conceptual. It was always music. Cats would leave the studio and go beat shopping, then hang in the park and look at other emcees or comedians: it was always artistry. We were around the making of *People's Instinctive Travels and the Paths of Rhythm*. I remember when they dropped the first single being so excited like my cousin's project just came out! Then Tribe went on to become Tribe. They are one of the most important groups in Hip-Hop history, forever. Period.

Till: Yeah, definitely. And shout out and rest in peace to Phife always.

Dres: Definitely rest in peace to Phife. And even Phife was (a) non-stop emcee. He was always attuned with being a better him. He was inspirational to me. To see Phife go from the first to the second album was amazing. I'm sure fans of music were like wow! We all saw it as important for us to become who we were supposed to become. Phife was about his work. He became the emcee he was supposed to be and that was inspiring.

Till: Dope. Okay, the next album is *De La Soul is Dead*.

Dres: Probably one of my favorite albums in Hip-Hop. For us to have been such a cool part of it was an amazing thing. It came at a time when we were working hard on our album. We used Calliope as well. Instead of three groups, it is four groups using Calliope. And the Beatnuts started using it toward the end of our time. All of us would be in each other's sessions. We are knee-deep in *A Wolf in*

Sheep's Clothing while they (De La) are working on *De La Soul is Dead.* They are starting to hear me as an emcee. They afford me the opportunity to jump on one of their tracks. It is the first song that anyone is ever hearing me on, "Fanatic of the B Word." Me doing that song was kind of like an arrival for me. It was an opportunity to be in the room. It was them saying, "You are a part of us. You're down. We accept you." It was a graduation of sorts. I was so happy any time I heard any record off that album. And Lawnge killed the skits! Everybody is a comedian, but Lawnge was able to find some really fine moments on tape. We were getting a lesson in so many ways on how we would go forward and create our project. We were flies on the wall and able to take it in and breathe it, and there was no pressure with it. They gave us the opportunity to sit at their dinner table and have a meal with them as brothers. I'll always love them for that. Me and Lawnge were kind of the last ones in the door, so to speak. We might not get put in the core group of De La, Tribe, and Jungle. But sometimes we should. We were right there when Tribe was working on *People's*. Lawnge did the cuts on "Buddy." We were right there. We had just got into the room. I feel like I came in and they were like, "close the door." And then the next generation came behind it. Or maybe we were the first of the next generation.

Till: I have to say, Dres, as we've been working on this book, we have talked to a lot of people. We asked all of them the same question, "Who are the Native Tongues? Who is the core?" and so far, everyone has mentioned the four groups - Jungle, De La Soul,

Tribe, and Black Sheep - and Monie Love and Queen Latifah. Everyone we've talked to so far has mentioned Black Sheep.

Dres: That's peace. I don't fight it. If anyone feels like the three groups are the base, you wouldn't be wrong. But anyone that would feel like there are four of us, you wouldn't be wrong either.

Till: So Native Tongues inspired and influenced a lot of people. I wanted to ask you about an album that I love. It is dope. It is *Theme + Echo = Krill* by the Legion.

Dres: The Legion are primarily self-produced. It was such a cool time for me but also a bittersweet time. To my understanding, I might have been one of the first emcees to get a label imprint. I get this imprint called One Love off the success of *A Wolf in Sheep's Clothing*. I really pushed for me to get this thing. I bring out the Legion and this female group called Emage out of Oakland. I had just offered the deal to Molecules. I wanted him to do a solo album. I used to bring him out during freestyles at shows, and he would always catch wreck. I was sold on him as a solo artist. He really wanted his crew to be a part of it. As he started producing and I'm seeing them (Dice and Smash and Molecules) grow as emcees, I kind of stepped back and let them do their own thing because I felt like they were capable. In getting this deal, I never wanted Lawnge to ever feel like he didn't have access to anything I was doing. I was so grateful for any opportunities that being in Black Sheep presented. I thought it would have been something we would have done together, but Lawnge and I were starting to go our own ways. I think success and money had a lot to do with that. It was what it was. I felt obligated to Lawnge because I never took for granted that I'm in the Native Tongues. I bumped into Lawnge who was going to be in the Native Tongues with or without me. Though I brought him into my house, he brought me into these sessions. I felt really obligated to him. Part of me felt like he felt a way because I had this deal, and he didn't have anything to do with it. So what I did was I made a deal with Lawnge, "I'd like to pay you $7,000 per track and every project I bring through One Love I need you to do 3 tracks on it. And in that way, you are always vested in whatever I'm doing out of loyalty. It was unfortunate that at that time. Emage - The Legion album, and our album (Non-Fiction), I thought if we dropped close to one another, we could tour together and do so many things in-house. That never got a chance to really happen because, not only did me and Lawnge end up having difficulties, but Polygram was about to be bought by Universal. A whole slew of stuff started happening to the degree that even the president of the label, Ed Eckstine, is becoming difficult about the Legion project, the Emage project. When the Black Sheep album came out, if you look at the spine of it, it says Black Sheep. When I saw that, I was like, "You know what, this sh*t is over, man." I was just like, before something horrible happens, I'm going to stop here and step back. I know myself much better than people's perception of me. I know for a fact I did the most intelligent thing. Which was just to step back. When I was at the pinnacle of Black Sheep's success, I was very much not at ease. I stepped back. I went down south and bought a crib in Carolina. I started my own independent thing. I did some of the things I wish the Natives had done. It's upsetting to me that, to this day, you can't write a check to the Native Tongues. I started learning. Sometimes, the mistake you make leads you to a place of safety. Sometimes, when something isn't for you, that winds up being a blessing.

Till: Your story reminds me of Shortie No Mass. We interviewed her recently, and she talked about a deal being all around her and it never worked out and she was actually happy. She saw an industry that she knew she wouldn't be happy in.

Dres: That's real. Sometimes, we get so caught up in our perception of something only to find out our perception was not the reality. I've discovered so many things that are so different than how I perceive them. Sometimes it's mind blowing. Especially as a Black man. To be Black is to have to find your way in the dark. There's not a lot of points of reference. There are not a lot of fathers that showed you. There's not a lot of examples in front of you. One of the things that happened with slavery was that for generations, you could be killed for reading. One thing we don't talk about that was equally as strong was that we did not have families. For generations, our families could be taken and sold to different places and killed and raped and maimed, whatever. It was the equivalent of having a field of cattle or a gate of pigs. You don't look at pigs like they are family, and you make sure the family stays together. That's literally how they looked at us. Generations down the road, some of our problems as a community is the lack of. The lack of family is probably one of the most tremendous things we don't speak about. Single mothers think that single mothering is something they are equipped to do. We are the only ones that feel like we can do it. Our children are proof that we can't. Our children don't have points of reference. A point of reference is so important. I've come to understand that, as I make sure I'm one to my sons. When I came up, without having a solid father figure, when I came into problems, I didn't have someone to reach out to. I didn't have an example that I remembered. I didn't have the things that a family unit brings to you navigating in a world full of problems. So we end up doing so many things by trial and error while other people with families have structure. They have an understanding, a hierarchy that they can remember when their father was in their position and what he did and what not to do. That is so important. One of the things that I think that Hip-Hop must address is how important the community needs family. It literally is going to cure so many of our ills when we start sacrificing for our families. It is so easy to walk away from someone that's just irritating you. Or they did something superficial that you feel goes against the grain. That's on both sides. Having a family is to sacrifice. It means something. It is worth something. We need generations of those sacrifices to be whole. Our music has to start speaking to that. The things that speak to us being whole - the Native Tongues were responsible for filling in some of those gaps. I'm disappointed in us to the degree that we weren't a microcosm of the thing we asked the people to be. Our example was very important, and it still is. I got a text from Tip, and it made me so happy. I'll DM Pos. I was mad at myself when Phife passed because I had been saying for like a month, "Give Phife a call, you haven't talked to Phife in a while." He passed and I was so mad for not just stopping and giving him a shout. We weren't a microcosm of the records we made. Of Black empowerment. Of us being a cohesive family. Of us having each other's back. We lost some of what we were supposed to do as we became successful. When we got to a space where all of us could stand on our own without needing the others, then that's what we did and that's what we do. And that's a horrible mistake.

iomos: Based on what you just said, do you think that's a systemic thing within the music industry? Is that a pattern that often happens? I'm thinking of Native Tongues, I'm thinking Wu-Tang. As you are climbing up the ladder, it's that cohesion, but then you reach success and that starts to put a strain on those relationships. Do you think that's intentional?

Dres: That's a brilliant question. Some of it lies in our inability to look at each other and see a brother first. To see a family member first. We are so broken down from a family unit, we will never give thought to bumping into a relative of ours if they weren't introduced from our mother or father, but they are there. We are related on so many levels. We have to see each other first before we see anyone else. We have to make sure we are good. That's what's been done to us all over the world. No one makes sure we are good. I don't mean this in a wrong way. If you are a gang member, we are not the OPS (Opposition). Gang members think other gang members are their OPS. No, your OPS are white supremacists. Your OPS are people that endanger the well-being of our community. So if you have the heart to aim the gun, have the sense to aim at the OP. I'm not advocating any form of violence, but if that's what you are doing, don't point it at the people behind you. If you really want to patrol the world, just know who your enemy is. That too is a Native Tongue voice.

iomos: Man, you are dropping gems all over the place. To me, Native Tongues is Ubuntu - I exist only because you exist. My existence is wrapped up in your existence. To me, that's what Native Tongues represented. There's no Tribe without Jungle Brothers, no De La without Black Sheep. That synergy that you all had between each other is definitely missing.

Dres: I know we are still getting older, and I see the grays. God is funny. You know how I know God has a sense of humor? (dramatic pause) Gray pubic hair (eruption of laughter). I still feel like a young dude. It takes these discussions. There is a hierarchy in everything I've learned. It doesn't stay the same. One of the things I learned in the Native Tongues is that any one of us could be at the top of the totem pole as far as people's perception (is concerned).

We all had an opportunity to be at the top. There are so many things you can do at the top of the totem pole that you can't do when you are at the middle or bottom. That I didn't realize until I wasn't at the top of the totem pole. I wish I had done a few things differently because I had a much better understanding of how to navigate. That being said, one of the things that inspires me to make music and get up in the morning and be a better me is that I'd like to revisit the totem pole before this is over. I'm the perfect person to have money at this point in my life because I'm already happy. It is not about me owning a Rolls Royce or fronting for anyone. It is about making moves and pooling my resources and being an example of what's possible when we do something together. But you can't do that unless you are able to look at others at the top of the totem poles in the eye. That's a good motivation for me. There are some things that are more important than the song itself. I'm looking for what the song can afford me. There are some statements I'd like to be able to make with the money. To make a purchase of character says a lot as opposed to frivolously spending money.

Till: That's dope. Man, you gave us a lot. Thank you. The impact of *A Wolf in Sheep's Clothing* and early Native Tongues albums is so profound. It put me on a course to pursue this music and this culture. I owe so much gratitude to the entire Native Tongues and to you, Dres. Thank you for being there and being a part of it and being so cool and down to earth with us. I really appreciate you and what you have given to us through the years.

Dres: I really appreciate it. We grow to become who we are supposed to be. We are not born who we are supposed to be. Let's keep growing. Your words all touched me sincerely. I hope that I'm an example of some of the things you spoke to in yourself. Y'all are going to get it. Just pass it forward. Everything you are, everything you become, you end up becoming a point of reference. You end up becoming a beacon, something that stands for something that should be standing. Once you discover that within yourself, you should grow. Once you discover in yourself what it is, your head never sees the ground from there. From there, you stand firm in that. When people see you, let them see the reflection of just that. I challenge y'all to be everything you are supposed to be. And y'all definitely seem to be on the right road. I appreciate y'all, and I appreciate the time and I hope to continue being who I'm supposed to be.

iomos: Well said, bro.

Till: As always, on that note we say, peace!

CHAPTER THIRTY-FIVE

Live Interview with Shortie No Mass

As conducted by Jay Hill

Jay Hill: So my friend MC Till, who runs the Everybody's Hip-Hop Label here in Cincy, hit me up last week and told me they wanted to interview you for their book on the Native Tongues and then he said, "Hey, but we think we have a way to get in contact with Shortie No Mass." And I'm like, "Excuse me?!" I'm very excited to be able to talk to you.

Shortie No Mass: Oh, cool.

Jay Hill: First off, how have you been?

Shortie No Mass: Good, busy. I'm all over the place. I literally just had to run back here to do this, so busy but good, great.

Jay Hill: Nice. So, would you say you're busy with music? Or just life stuff overall?

Shortie No Mass: I have my own company. I own properties. So, I have one that I had to get the cleaning lady in, another one after I get off of this. I have to check and see how the construction is going. So...

Jay Hill: Nice.

Shortie No Mass: Yeah, that's my other love.

Jay Hill: All right. Well, congratulations on that. How long have you been doing it?

Shortie No Mass: Mm, seven years.

Jay Hill: Nice. And you've been able to push it through the pandemic and everything?

Shortie No Mass: Mm-hmm. It was scary, but actually, I made a lot of money during the pandemic.

Jay Hill: Wow. Now, there are a lot of little secret blessings that came through (the pandemic.) It's certainly not a good thing, but a lot of people, when given that opportunity to focus and just be at home for a bit, if you wanted to be in your home, took advantage.

Shortie No Mass: It was definitely scary. I closed on a property, we had a closing date and the world was literally shutting down, and I was like, "Should we be buying this right now?" We just weren't sure, because people were losing their jobs, or... So, it was fine, it was totally okay. There's some people and I guess, depending on the industry you were in, some people were really okay. And others were really not.

Jay Hill: Oh yeah. So, I've been trying to be a full-time musician for a while, and I was working retail. So, at that time, they found a way to get us working from home. I wanted to... but, since they had us back home, I found the opportunity to just start focusing on music again and making music, because for a while, I would go to work, go to practice, go to a show, go to work, go to a show, go to work, go to a show. I didn't really have to do none of that for a while.

Shortie No Mass: Yeah.

Jay Hill: I wonder where and when did you get the inspiration to get active with Hip-Hop again? And get started on *Here Goes Nothing?*

Shortie No Mass: So, I don't make any money from Hip-Hop. I never have. I'm a hustler, so I'm always going to chase a check, just for life. You know what I mean? I have to provide. So, Hip-Hop never really showed me love from that financial perspective. I could never make it my first priority. It's a love but not a priority. "Like This", I recorded in '95-ish. Somebody put that on YouTube, it got caught into an algorithm. It was nuts during the pandemic, because I think a lot of people did have time to focus on finding new music and listening and all of that.

Jay Hill: Oh, yeah.

Shortie No Mass: And it was at two million (views), right before the pandemic. And literally, now it's at 10 million. So, in the last two years, and this is a song from 1995. So, it was like, "Whoa." And it was new fans and it was old fans. And I think with music, for me, I would always have friends who did music. And if they'd ask me to be on a project, I would totally support them and help them. I never focused on my own project, but I started to see that I came from an old school music industry mentality that people over a certain age don't go into the industry. All that is out the window nowadays.

Jay Hill: Yeah.

Shortie No Mass: You know what I mean? Now, it doesn't matter. With streaming services, they've made access to everybody.

Jay Hill: If you're dope, somebody's going to find you.

Shortie No Mass: Absolutely. But, if you come from back in the day, where you had a deal and that's the only way people heard you and you think they only put (out) and support younger artists, then you sometimes can get stuck in that mentality as an older artist. This YouTube video showed me that I still had fans and I also had new fans. People who had never even heard of me were like, "Oh my God, who's this?" And I was like, "Well, what's the difference if I became a new artist that just came out yesterday? There's clearly still a fan base for me, new and old."

Jay Hill: For sure.

Shortie No Mass: So I felt like, "Okay, if you're still asking me for an album after 20 years, I owe it to you." And now, I have this new fan base that's like, "She's dope. I want to hear more." So again, what you said resonates with me, because I had time to focus on doing the album. There were things going on, but it wasn't as much going on, because everything was shut down. So, that's when I wrote, that's when I had more time to just chill and focus. And if I'm going to do it, let me do it now, because I have time to do it. At this point it's, "Here goes nothing." Because I didn't have (anything) to lose, because if it didn't do good, I'm okay. If it does do good, I'm okay. I had nothing to lose. So, that's how *Here Goes Nothing* came about.

Jay Hill: That's dope. I am curious when were the beats made? Because, they sounded new, but definitely with old school craft in mind at the same time. And I saw that you were working with the Beatminerz again, like you did for "Like This".

Shortie No Mass: Right. That the album's funny. So, the label re-released one of my singles, "Like This"/"You Like My Style", and they sold out.

Jay Hill: Yeah.

Shortie No Mass: At the same time, this was 2019. So, the label was like, "We want an album." And I was like, "I don't know about an album. That's a lot. I'll give you an EP. I could definitely do an EP." So, I focused on the EP and that was all new songs. So I said, "Well, let me just use the Beatminerz. It was easy. And it was a sound people had already liked because they did stuff before. So, that was new stuff." And then, I was going through, organizing everything, and I found all these old tracks that I had already recorded in 2007 I never used. So I said, well, since I never used these, I might as well use them now (and) throw them on an album.

Jay Hill: We'll tweak them and also Evil Dee from Beatminerz, he had the sessions still.

Jay Hill: Oh, that's really cool.

Shortie No Mass: That's how it became an album. It was so convenient. And it was so funny because his brother, Walt, was like, "He doesn't have them." And he was like, "Yes, I do." And Walt was like, "That was 2007. He doesn't have them." And he was like, "Yes, I do." And he found them and he had them. So, we didn't know if it was going to work, but it worked. Now, it's interesting you say, "It sounds like a lot of new beats." Because a lot of the beats that I used from 2007 were very futuristic. I always felt like they were ahead of their time and they're actually from 2007.

Jay Hill: Which ones were those? Because, I mean, if you don't mind me saying, I really dug "Tragic Charade" and "Can't Get Enough of Me". Those tracks really went hard.

Shortie No Mass: Okay. So, "Tragic Charade" is new. But it's done by a younger (producer), Walt's son. He's in his early 20s. So, that's more of a younger vibe. "Can't Get Enough of Me," is 2007.

Jay Hill: Wow. What about "Inspiration"?

Shortie No Mass: 2007.

Jay Hill: 2007? That one was hard. I like that one.

Shortie No Mass: Mm-hmm. "Inspiration", "Can't Get Enough of Me", and "Identity Crisis".

Jay Hill: Okay cool.

Shortie No Mass: But see now, they're not Beatminerz. They're J-Zone beats. I always felt like J-Zone gave me a different sound that was always ahead of his time.

Jay Hill: Yeah, yeah.

Shortie No Mass: And now, yeah, they're 2007 beats. Songs, the whole thing was recorded and everything.

Jay Hill: That's really tight. And then, you still managed to prove from there, you've like still got it, but-

Shortie No Mass: Yeah, I guess I did. Okay, thank you.

Jay Hill: I do want to say congratulations on that.

Shortie No Mass: Thank you.

Jay Hill: But, taking things back. How do you think you've changed, as a person and as an artist, since we first heard you on The Roots album and with De La Soul?

Shortie No Mass: As a person and probably as an artist too, I'm way more confident now. I mean, I'm older. So, I really don't care what people think about me. There's a lot to be said for that though. Because I think that when you're young, you aren't as comfortable in yourself.

Jay Hill: This is very true.

Shortie No Mass: Yeah. And I mean, I have a family, they love me, whether I rap, I don't rap, am young, or old. So, I feel when you get older, you're comfortable and it's a comfort and a freedom and you don't care what people think. So, that definitely helps in music, because I don't care what you think. I'm just going to put it out and (if) you like it, you like it. If you don't, it's not for you. And that's okay.

Jay Hill: Yeah. That's tight. What do you think a Shortie No Mass album would've sounded like if you'd released it in 2000?

Shortie No Mass: Well, I was actually signed at Def Jam. Or, I was about to sign with Def Jam in '93. So actually, my first album would've probably come out '94, '95. I was supposed to be on that first Violator Def Jam, like the Warren G/Foxy Brown era. So, I probably would've come out then. I think I would've had a dope album. I think Chris Lighty would've made sure we had all the stops to make a classic album. I think more opportunities would've come and back then, that was old music industry stuff. So, I would've gotten crazy opportunities. But now (that I'm) older, I don't think that's the path I would've wanted to take. I'm okay. People ask me, "Are you upset that you didn't put an album out? Or, you didn't sign to Def Jam?" And mm-mm. I don't think I was supposed to, just to who I am as a person.

Jay Hill: Yeah.

Shortie No Mass: I hate the industry. I really don't like it.

Jay Hill: The industry's not really built for people who want to make their own way and say what they want to say all the time.

Shortie No Mass: And I think less now, because there's more opportunities to be independent-

Jay Hill: Mm-hmm.

Shortie No Mass: But I think back then, it was sheisty and everyone was trying to get over on everyone. And I think I would've found myself successful but really angry. I don't know how those experiences would've shaped who I am. I'm okay with that.

Jay Hill: Yeah. That's wise. I respect that. Going back to the '90s, I notice when I check out interviews from A Tribe Called Quest or even recently from Dante Ross, who's doing stuff with Open Mike Eagle right now and talking about his time working with Tommy Boy, everyone seems to have a different definition of Native Tongues. And I want to know what Native Tongues is to you?

Shortie No Mass: Native Tongues for me honestly, I was a fan of Native Tongues, because you have to understand, Native Tongues had dissolved right before I got down with De La. So, I'm not an official Native Tongues member. I'm an affiliate.

Jay Hill: So wait, what would you say is the line between a member and an affiliate? If you don't mind me asking.

Shortie No Mass: I think it's easy to lump everyone into De La, Tribe, Black Sheep, all that and say that era and the collective is Native Tongues. But it wasn't a thing when I came on board. It wasn't. Now, I still met everyone because I was in that same circle of people. But, as a Native Tongue thing, it was before my time. So I don't know what the specifics are, but Native Tongues wasn't a thing when I did De La's album.

Jay Hill: Okay.

Shortie No Mass: I don't know. It's tricky. Do I know Monie? Yes. Do I know Latifah? Yes. Do I know Jungle Brothers? Yes. Do I know Tribe? Of course. Do I know everyone in Native Tongues? Of course, I have interactions. If I run into them today, it's "Hey, what's up?" But it wasn't a thing when I got with them. It wasn't like, "Oh, this is the Native Tongues crew." No.

Jay Hill: Okay. Yeah, I noticed people didn't rep it super, super hard on albums. They weren't trying to make, "Hey, this is Native Tongues merch. You got to be like this to be a native. You got to-"

Shortie No Mass: Yeah, so all I can say is this: outside looking in - and this has been confirmed by people - there are a lot of strong personalities in that Native Tongues collective, mainly the men. That, at some point (it) didn't work. That was a problem as some members of Native Tongues, mainly just because of the industry and the time, got more successful than other members in Native Tongues. But, when you have strong personalities who think they are leaders and they start this and they didn't do that and I'm this and I'm that, then people butt heads, I think, from my perspective, that was the downfall of that. But I came after that.

Jay Hill: Okay. Okay. So, what would you say was your experience, even just working with De La on your own?

Shortie No Mass: It was dope. I was so young, was 16, 17. I was in high school. It was interesting to be in the studio all the time and just see how they were. I had been in a studio, a real studio, but it was just interesting to see the way that they did stuff. I mean, I went to mastering sessions with Bob Power. So, I was there for the bulk of everything. And it was dope. Just, it was different. You had a label and you had a marketing team and you had trips to the label and promotional tours and regular tours and photo shoots and rehearsals at SIR, so I definitely got the official artist experience.

Jay Hill: That's really cool.

Shortie No Mass: And I'm glad I came with a group like De La. Listen, there were a lot of dope groups in the '90s, right? But De La had an international appeal, which gave me an international appeal by default. I could have been with a dope ass group, but maybe I wouldn't have had the reach in the world that De La gave me.

Jay Hill: And then, even then, you were talking about how the industry was real sheisty at the time. So, for De La to be the Hip-Hop group you come out

	with, and for you to be 17, still a young girl, able to represent yourself the way you wanted to, at that time, is still really bold.
Shortie No Mass:	Well, I will say this. Of all the groups that I could have come out with, De La, Tribe, they were good guys. They were good human beings. So I was the only girl on tour, and I was 18. No one was ever disrespectful to me. They were good people. They were very respectful, they were raised right. Let's say that. I can imagine there were other groups that I could have come out with that I would have probably had a whole different experience as a woman by myself, a young girl by myself. So, I was good from a safety perspective.
Jay Hill:	Yeah.
Shortie No Mass:	I was good. When I say the industry is sheisty, the industry is sheisty, but it's in a beautiful box with nice ribbon and wrapping paper.
Jay Hill:	Yeah. That's how they get you.
Shortie no Mass:	100%.
Jay Hill:	For sure.
Shortie No Mass:	When I say it's sheisty, it's not a bad atmosphere to be in, but you're getting got during that niceness. You know what I mean? So, I always liken it to the Death Row days. They'll keep your royalties, but they'll buy you a Bentley. So, a lot of us are like, "Ooh, he bought me a Bentley. And he bought me a Rolls Royce. That's great." But is

it great? When they're keeping licensing rights and publishing rights and... So, it's pretty and fun and happy...But, it's not... That's the way they do it.

Jay Hill: Considering the artistic landscape of '93, '94, '95 and the environment that you were in, I want to ask where you think you've seen the influence of De La Soul, the Native Tongues Movement, and even yourself, pop up in culture since then?

Shortie No Mass: Since then? I don't know. I mean, I just feel like obviously with music, especially Hip-Hop, really mainly Hip-Hop, it's very indicative of the times we live in, right?

Jay Hill: Yeah.

Shortie No Mass: So, is there an influence now? Maybe, I don't know. I'm sure. J. Cole maybe. I don't know what inspires him, but it wouldn't be a far stretch to say he was inspired by listening to a Tribe album or whatever. But I just think that music then, music in between and music now, is always going to be representative of an African American culture.

Jay Hill: Yeah.

Shortie No Mass: You know what I mean? And that's more of the influence. I don't know if De La has an influence today. It's nostalgic, is that influential? It's nostalgic, but I don't know if it's influential. Taking my son to see Spider-Man and hearing "Three Is The Magic Number." That's nostalgic. Is it influential? I don't know.

Jay Hill: I will say, maybe, it's because I'm like a nerd, but I listen to a whole lot of underground Hip-Hop.

Shortie No Mass: I'm a nerd. I'm a super nerd.

Jay Hill: Oh, for sure.

Shortie No Mass: I'm a super nerd. I'm an official nerd.

Jay Hill: Tight.

Shortie No Mass: I build Legos. I'm a nerd, nerd.

Jay Hill: So, I don't have Legos, but... and I guess this won't be quite as nerdy for you, but as a 26-year-old in the Year of Our Lord 2022, I really love tape machines. I got a duplicator over on the floor over there. I'm trying to start a tape label out of my room.

Shortie No Mass: Listen. And that's what's dope and maybe that's my answer. I feel like De La, the culture from the '80s, the '90s is a lane for younger kids today to be dope, but different. And not do the same thing as everyone else.

Jay Hill: And you all were really, really, really bold with that. At the time, a lot of people were going gangster and people in your realm were just saying, "No, I'm just doing my thing. There's a lot happening, or happening around me, but I'm just doing me." And-

Shortie No Mass: Well, so again, I talk about trends. Jungle Brothers were house music, right? Earthy. And then, it went into conscious rap, and then it was about EPMD. It was just about, just being positive and having fun, or even being militant like Public Enemy, right? But it was all positive. It was a positive message for African Americans. Then, you got into gangster rap, NWA got dope after that, right?

Jay Hill: Yeah.

Shortie No Mass: And again, they're speaking on what their life reflects. Then, you get into Jay-Z, Puffy right after that. '95 is that Bad Boy era. It's still dope rhymes and dope beats, but it's more sexy and shiny and pop bottles and have fun, right?

Jay Hill: Mm-hmm.

Shortie No Mass: And then, you go into down South music, more like the South guys-

Jay Hill: Yeah. We got real Southern around the mid 2000s. And then-

Shortie No Mass: Exactly, right? So, then you got real Southern. And then I think from Southern you got into this genre of music which is again, representative of these kids' lives-

Jay Hill: Yeah, it is.

Shortie No Mass: But look at our economy, look at our culture, look at our world. You can follow that trend. So, Hip-Hop is only reflective of the times of people's actual day-to-day lives.

Jay Hill: One of the most literal artistic reports of any given period, because no other genre is this wordy.

Shortie No Mass: Right.

Jay Hill: People are stating how they feel, as a result of the world around them, in real time and in full sentences.

Shortie No Mass: Absolutely.

Jay Hill: The music behind it is a gift. That's something to remember it by…

Shortie No Mass: It is.

Jay Hill: …but is so very real.

Shortie No Mass: So reflective of the times.

Jay Hill: So before we go, I wanted to share about this label called Greedhead from the 2010s. They had this group Das Racist that spearheaded a blatantly nerdy rap movement. It's like the 90s movement was Afrocentric while the 2010s was about being intersectional. It was the first time I saw an Indian man with multi-racial individuals, Black, Cuban, Jewish. They are talking about their racial struggles and the life in New York post 9/11 as a brown person, being black and being mixed and not really being taken seriously as a black person, but still having all this knowledge of your own culture and more than the people who don't want you to claim it, have on their own.

Shortie No Mass: Mm-hmm.

Jay Hill: And they had a lot of references to De La Soul-type stuff. And they were often compared to De La Soul at the time. There's even a "Das Racist is Dead" article.

Shortie No Mass: Oh wow. So, they really were.

Jay Hill: Yeah. I think you might dig them because you're into some really abstract imagery in your verses. You were on some more bugged-out styles, and I really dig that. That's very much my wheelhouse. So one, thank you for helping pioneer that stuff. And two, Das Racist is definitely just that for an hour.

Shortie No Mass: Oh, okay. Well, I'll definitely pull them up and check them out.

Jay Hill: Dang, I should be telling you about my own music, haha but nah. Actually, if I've taken up enough of your time, that is just about everything I wanted to cover. I really do appreciate you getting on Zoom with me and being part of this.

Shortie No Mass: Yeah, definitely. It was a pleasure speaking with you.

Jay Hill: It was great speaking with you!

THE NATIVE TONGUES REVIEW

Part Five
Written Interviews

CHAPTER THIRTY-SIX

Written Interview with Chip Fu

Questions submitted by MC Till (with help from the crew)

Till: What was your introduction to the Native Tongues and what was your role in it?

Chip Fu: The connection came from us being one of the first groups that Tribe produced for. Not only that, having Latifah for management and production from Dres from Black Sheep made it seem like we were the group that the Natives were working on.

Till: How did the collaboration with Phife come about on "La Schmoove"?

Chip Fu: Well, we were working with Ali, and we always spoke about doing a song together with Phife, and this song just felt right.

Till: How did you get together with Shaq? Are you all still cool?

Chip Fu: Yes, till this day, we are still cool. We heard we were his favorite rap group at the time, and the Flavor Unit hooked it up for us to meet. When we met, we vibed like we all knew each other for a minute. Then we decided to go to the studio, and he

	dropped an incredible verse. From there, history was made.
Till:	Being that you and the Fu-Schnickens included martial arts in your music, did you ever get compared to the Wu-Tang Clan? If so, did it feel like a compliment? A diss? Other?
Chip Fu:	We never was compared. We were only asked who came out first with the martial arts influence and that would be us. But Wu-Tang did it differently than us and secured their spot as legends in the game. I'm a fan of their music. Plus, before us, the Beastie boys wore Asian gis in their promo pictures.
Till:	Who was your favorite producer to work with back then? Who is your favorite producer today?
Chip Fu:	Back then, Ali. Today, Ali and Pete Rock/Preemo.
Till:	If you could go back to the mid 90s and make an album with any Native Tongues member, who would it be and why?
Chip Fu:	Well, it would just be Phife and myself 'cause we had planned on doing an album before he transitioned. We called ourselves BQE (Brooklyn Queens Expressway). We only did one song together at the time called "Rumors." It was a song to hush all the critics that were talking about Tribe.
Till:	Wow! That's dope. So part of Native Tongues seemed to be all about community and naturally collaborating on music. Do you see something

similar to the Native Tongues happening today? If not, do you think it is needed?

Chip Fu: Only the Dungeon Family and Wu-Tang remind me of the Native Tongue collective by everybody collabing with their crew making incredible records. Now when you hear those types of records today with these new groups, it sounds like it was only done for business. Back then, you can tell it was about the music because of how the records came out.

Till: If you were assigned to create a next generation Native Tongues Crew from new artists of the past decade or so, who would you choose and why?

Chip Fu: Cordae, J-Cole, and Kendrick for the obvious reason. First off, they can rhyme. Not only that, they seem to be the voices of this new generation, and they all have a balance; they can cover all topics when it comes to song structure.

Till: Switching gears here a bit. Being from Trinidad, can you touch upon the impact Caribbean culture has had on Hip-Hop culture from your perspective?

Chip Fu: Some of your best artists are from the West Indies or have West Indian lineage, from Biggie to Busta to KRS and Red Alert and the list goes on. The sound systems from the West Indies had a big influence on the park jams in NYC, especially with Kool Herc being from Jamaica.

Till: You had incredible success in the 90s. What inspired you to do your art back then? What inspires you today?

Chip Fu: Back then, what inspired me was making my family proud and being able to help my parents. What inspires me today is I feel I have a lot more things to cover musically that I didn't display.

Till: Do you still keep in touch with Poc Fu and Moc Fu? What is your relationship with them like in 2022?

Chip Fu: Yes I do, and we cool. Those are my brothers.

Till: For people who followed you and were fans of you back in the 90s, what would you want them to know about you that they might not know?

Chip Fu: I constantly challenged myself when it came to writing. I always wanted to try new things, and when I did, the company (Jive Records) didn't allow it; they wanted me to just play my role in the group.

Till: What are you working on now?

Chip Fu: I have a solo album that I'm finishing up called *ROYAL BLOOD*. It's an incredible piece of work that I can't wait for people to hear. I'm also working on re-launching my music school initiative called MAATH (Music Appreciation, Art, Time, and Healing).

Till: That's really dope! Thanks again for sharing some of yourself with us today. Is there anything else you'd like to add before we go?

Chip Fu: Follow me on Twitter, Instagram and Facebook @chipfu and keep God first.

Till: Peace!

CHAPTER THIRTY-SEVEN

Written Interview with Masta Ace

Questions submitted by Profound (with help from the crew)

Profound: When was the first time you heard about the Native Tongues? What did you think about them when you first heard about them?

Masta Ace: I don't remember hearing the term Native Tongues until after the "Buddy" video and the magazine cover they did. I was already a fan of all of them individually. For the first time I was seeing them as a collective.

Profound: Did you ever feel like the Juice Crew and Native Tongues were in competition or was it always love and respect? Or a little bit of both? Like when their albums dropped, did it feel like colleagues or competition?

Masta Ace: I never felt competition with JC and NT...to me, the production, songs and lyrics were in two different lanes. They were definitely viewed by me as peers.

Profound: What did the Native Tongues mean to you? What did you learn from them? How did they inspire you?

Masta Ace: For me, it all started with Tribe in 1990... the *People's Instinctive...* album was groundbreaking for me. The production and songs were so different from anything at the time. It showed me that an artist didn't have to be stuck in a box. They broke all the rules of that time. De La came along and put an exclamation point on that theory. They dared to be different, and that's what gave me the courage to just be different than what was out there.

Profound: Do you have a favorite Native Tongues member? Or simply an emcee from the crew that really connected to you?

Masta Ace: Me and Phife had sports in common. Whenever we talked, it was about football and basketball. I was more a football guy, and he was more into basketball. But his knowledge of other sports was beyond mine. We both wore jerseys a lot before the whole throwback craze took over. I remember having the opportunity to be managed by Flavor Unit/Shakim and deciding to go another direction. I often wonder, had I done that, how I would be viewed today. Who knows what music would have come from that relationship, what albums, collaborations would have happened. Would I be considered NT or JC? It's interesting to think about.

Profound: Have you ever recorded a song with any of the Native Tongues members? If not, who would you most like to do a song with and why?

Masta Ace: I never have but.... See my previous answer. Lol

Profound: How do you feel about the Native Tongues' impact on Hip-Hop?

Masta Ace: The impact is huge and undeniable. NT proved Hip-Hop isn't just one thing. It's not just gold chains, Dapper Dan and Mercedes Benzes… it's made up of multiple layers, styles and voices. They made it okay to be "other than." They gave birth to the Kendrick Lamars and J. Coles IMO.

Profound: What is your favorite Native Tongue album and why?

Masta Ace: It's a tie between ATCQ's *The Low End Theory* and De La Soul's *3 Feet High*... Both those albums helped shape who I became as an artist.

Profound: If the Native Tongues decided to make an album today and asked you to executive produce it, what would you do? Who would you have produce it? One producer? Many? Which producers? Would you have guest emcees? Who?

Masta Ace: The album should be produced by Q-Tip, Kanye, and Hi-Tek! Guests would be Kendrick, Cole, André 3000, and Rapsody.

Profound: That sounds dope! Thank you for your time and stories, Masta Ace. We really appreciate you!

CHAPTER THIRTY-EIGHT

Written Interview with Phat Hentoff about Raw Deluxe *by Jungle Brothers*

Questions by MC Till

Till: Peace, Phat Hentoff. Before we dig into *Raw Deluxe*, it is only right to ask, what's your favorite Native Tongues album of all time and what's your favorite Jungle Brothers album (if they are different)?

Phat Hentoff: Well, I could give you my top 3 a lot easier, but if I had to say my absolute favorite, it's A Tribe Called Quest's *Beats, Rhymes & Life*. My favorite Jungle Brothers album is *Done By The Forces Of Nature*.

Till: Where does *Raw Deluxe* fit into your favorite Jungle Brothers albums?

Phat Hentoff: It would have to be my 3rd favorite, right after *Straight Out The Jungle*.

Till: Do you remember where you were and what you were doing when you first heard *Raw Deluxe*?

Phat Hentoff: Crazy, but I didn't hear the album until around 2004. I believe I found a CD copy at CD

	Warehouse, and it was only 2 or 3 dollars. Took a chance, as I often did back then, and picked it up. I know I wasn't expecting much, but I was instantly digging it.
Till:	What captured you about this album? What stood out?
Phat Hentoff:	First thing was the cover. Simple but dope. I think the standout thing about the album as a whole is the hooks. If a verse was ever a little lackluster, the hook brought you back. The production doesn't slack either.
Till:	Where does this album fit in your favorite albums from that year of 1997? When you think about this album, what other albums from that era come to mind?
Phat Hentoff:	I don't know where it would fit in with all the other releases of 1997, but it's on the list…and that says a lot cuz '97 had joints (IMO). *Life After Death, Wu-Tang Forever, Stone Crazy, Funcrusher Plus, When Disaster Strikes, One Day It Will All Make Sense, Jurassic 5*….
Till:	This album doesn't seem to get a lot of recognition. Do you sense that too? Why do you think that is?
Phat Hentoff:	I've discussed it with other heads, and I can't recall anyone agreeing with me, haha. There are some for-sure duds on the album and maybe that turned people off, but when they get it right, it hits. I think they possibly lost a chunk of their

audience after *J Beez Wit The Remedy* (I dig that album, too) and listeners just stopped checking for them. No radio play back then wasn't doing them any favors either.

Till: What do you think is Jungle Brothers' most significant contribution to Hip-Hop?

Phat Hentoff: Being the first in the Native Tongues crew to start to bubble might be the biggest. I know they were instrumental in providing studio time to other members and using their connections to get the music out. Incorporating house music and blending it with Hip-Hop was major as well. Not being afraid to be creative.

Till: Turning back to the album, what's your favorite song? What is it about this song that makes it your favorite?

Phat Hentoff: "Moving Along" is my favorite. The hook!!!

Till: What do you think about the Native Tongues Remix of "How Ya Want It We Got It?" How does it size up to other Native Tongue posse cuts?

Phat Hentoff: It's right up there with the rest, I believe. The beat is tough, and I love how Tip sets it off. I don't think there were nearly enough posse cuts, so any time they did one, I was here for it.

Till: What does this album mean to you in 2022?

Phat Hentoff: I found a vinyl copy about 4 years ago. I don't keep records in my collection if I don't listen to

	them, so that's how I judge what the music means to me. No matter what year, dope is dope. Writing this makes me want to relisten now!
Till:	Before you do that, is there anything else you'd like to add about this album?
Phat Hentoff:	The biggest thing is give it a shot. There are 5 or 6 really strong tracks on the album that listeners would be surprised by.
Till:	Thanks so much for taking the time to chat with us. And thanks for all the dope album and book covers!
Phat Hentoff:	I enjoy doing them and what you brothers do for the culture. Thanks for including me.

CHAPTER THIRTY-NINE

Written Interview with Wordsworth

Questions by Profound (with help from MC Till)

Profound: Peace, Wordsworth. Thanks so much for taking time to share your reflections on the Native Tongues. I always looked at you as being of the Native Tongues lineage. Do you see yourself that way?

Wordsworth: I think plenty of us were influenced by Native Tongues because of how eclectic they were. They had a quality mix of messages that motivated different regions. There was a positive, fun vibe, with tales of social and street issues.

Profound: Can you tell us about your first time hearing the Native Tongues? What was the first song or album that spoke to you from the crew? Why do you think that particular piece of music engaged you?

Wordsworth: Well, I'm a big fan of Tribe, Latifah, and De La Soul, and when the song "Buddy" came out, that's when I realized what Native Tongues meant. The support they showed each other was great to see. Also, can't forget the Jungle Brothers. I was engaged by the music because of the fun that anyone could relate to. "Bonita Applebum", "Ladies First", "I'll House You", all depend on the year order.

Profound: When did you first meet members of the collective? Who did you meet first and what was that like?

Wordsworth: I met Q-Tip first after he hosted a Lyricist Lounge event that me and Punch performed at. After that performance, days later, we heard Q-Tip wanted to meet us and that's how we ended up on *The Love Movement*. It was dope because we had mutual friends, Mos Def and Kweli. We felt like we were validated.

Profound: What do you think their presence in Hip-Hop meant in the late 80s, early 90s?

Wordsworth: Their presence meant diversity of styles, flow, content, production, and dressing. You were able to identify with each of them from different perspectives. There was a message in their music, and it was accepted and respected.

Profound: September 29th, 1998, was a great day for Hip-Hop with the release of *The Love Movement & Black Star*. I'm sure that was a great day for you too, as you were featured on both albums. What was that day like for you?

Wordsworth: Those two albums have and will keep my career extended. I just was excited for people to hear me and see if I impressed them and lived up to the expectations. I was excited, but only the supporters can validate what I do, and they did. I was so young that I was excited, in college, and just still wondering what would come of it.

Profound: I started this interview asking you about how you see yourself in relation to the Native Tongues. In addition to you, I also saw/see Yasiin Bey and Talib Kweli and Common and The Roots and others as descendants of the Native Tongues. To you, what makes an artist or group remind you of the Native Tongues? And who are some newer artists that give you Native Tongue vibes?

Wordsworth: I think the effect is rippled through messages and music that has resonated with the world. J. Cole, Kendrick, Cordae, each have something from that era, knowingly and maybe unknowingly. Sometimes, the essence or origin resurfaces without the realization of its beginning but evolves to what we hear today.

Profound: If you could have been a fly on the wall for the recording of any one Native Tongue album, which album would it be and why?

Wordsworth: It would have to be *Midnight Marauders*. That's a perfect album. The production and concepts were on point. Would've liked to see how the concepts were created.

Profound: If you could get the entire collective together and executive produce an album for them, who would you bring in to produce it? One producer? Several? Who?

Wordsworth: You have to have Q-Tip do it. He's a mastermind and simply brilliant with flavor when crafting. Also, he has experience DJing, so I think he understands the current climate and can maintain the integrity of the past.

Profound: Who would you personally like to make music with from the collective that you have not gotten to work with yet?

Wordsworth: An entire album produced by Q-Tip. We were supposed to sign to his label before *The Love Movement*. So would've been dope to have an entire project produced by him.

Profound: Do you think the Native Tongues are properly documented? Do you think there is enough material written and recorded about them now to ensure their legacy lives on say in 30, 40, 50 years? If not, what do you think needs to be done to ensure their legacy remains relevant and meaningful?

Wordsworth: They need an Unsung or documentary. I think certain groups have songs that will go on for generations but unsure if the Native Tongues title will be brought up unless we continuously document it like now.

Big shoutout to Wordsworth for taking the time to share his Native Tongues thoughts with us. His album with Pearl Gates produced by Quincy Tones made it to #3 in our first volume of *The Boom Bap Review* book. It is an incredible and authentic piece of music that weaves together boom bap sensibilities with mass appeal.

Check it out and all of Wordsworth's music. You won't be disappointed.

CHAPTER FORTY

Written Interview with Dug Infinite
Questions by MC Till & Profound

MC Till: Peace, Dug Infinite! This is MC Till and I'm a huge fan of your work. Thanks for taking the time to chat with us about your influence regarding the Native Tongues.

Dug Infinite: Thank you so much for reaching out, it's an honor!

Till: I'd like to first ask you about one of my favorite albums from the mid '90s, *Accept Your Own and Be Yourself* by No I.D. featuring you all over it and Infamous Syndicate on several tracks. To me, this album has a very Native Tongues vibe. Do you see it that way?

Dug Infinite: I never thought of it that way until now, but I guess when you think of producers that rhyme, record dig, DJ, B-boy, and showcase female emcees, it is easier to make a connection to a Native Tongues type of vibe.

Till: Can you describe what a Native Tongues vibe is to you?

Dug Infinite: I would advocate that the sound created the vibe. The sound was unique, and the members of that crew were known for making that sound popular to the masses. The movement was a vibe too. It was diverse, earthy, conscious yet urban.

Till: Staying on the *Accept Your Own* topic, was that a brainchild of No I.D. and you played a supporting role? Or was it more of a co-created album?

Dug Infinite: That was a No I.D. brainchild. It was his record deal. We collaborated freely back in those days because we were pushing each other to be the best we could be at chopping beats. Peter Kang, the A&R at the label, got me involved in the album after we did "The Real Weight." He got me paid to leave a construction project so I went to No I.D.'s studio every day instead.

Till: What does this album mean to you decades later?

Dug Infinite: It still has the same value it had to me when it was created. That was very important in establishing a production sound that came from the south side of Chicago. We were only known for emceeing back then, but that album spotlighted production because we were producers.

Till: One last question about that album. You and Syndicate were great on that album. Do either of you have unreleased music that will ever see the light of day (my fingers are crossed as I'm typing this, hahaha)?

THE NATIVE TONGUES REVIEW

Dug Infinite: Thanks! Hahaha, yeah man. We certainly can't take it with us, and there is so much unreleased music we did. It was all sample-based back then, so let's hope sample clearance gets streamlined in the future. That would help get that stuff out faster and get everyone properly paid.

Till: I'm hoping! Okay, now onto more Native Tongue questions. Do you remember the first time you heard a song or album by any of the Native Tongue members? Can you tell us about that experience?

Dug Infinite: Yep! The Jungle Brothers *Straight out the Jungle.* "I'm Gonna Do You" was my joint. I had a green Suzuki Jeep with (4) 12-inch woofers and (4) 6x9s with some Rockford Fosgate amps, and I used to blast that album all over the city.

Till: Having worked closely with Common, did you ever see him as a Native Tongues member? Or maybe a descendant of the collective? Do you have an idea of how Common saw himself in that regard?

Dug Infinite: Ha! Only he could answer that, but I think around the time, doing "The Bizness" with De La Soul, there was a clear connection. The Lyricist Lounge sessions and his single "1999/Like They Use To Say" on Rawkus with Hi-Tek and me was another time where it seemed like that was the case. Then of course, there is the J Dilla, Tribe, and Common connection.

Till: If you could produce an album for any Native Tongues member, who would it be and why?

Dug Infinite: I've done songs with a few of the members before, but I'm going to cheat here and say all of them! Native Tongues reunion album and the reason why is because I could showcase a wide range of production styles.

Till: Dope, dope. Okay, I'm going to throw it over to our guy Profound for a few more questions. Profound, take it away.

Profound: Peace, Jedi Master Dug Infinite!! Thank you for taking a few minutes to answer these questions.

Dug Infinite: You're welcome, Profound.

Profound: Being that we are both from Chicago, do you feel there is a "Chicago Sound," and would you say you are one of the originators of that sound?

Dug Infinite: Yes, there are definitely a few sounds! I know that I created the sped-up soul sound with the voices, but the original production styles are out there in history if people listen to how the beats sounded from the first releases to how and when they progressed. You can see the originators that way too.

Profound: How is the Chicago sound comparable to the Native Tongue sound?

Dug Infinite: I don't think there is one specific Chicago sound, so it would be difficult for me to make that comparison.

Profound: Gotcha. Being a fan of the Native Tongues collective, I'm wondering what is your favorite Native Tongue album?

Dug Infinite: *Midnight Marauders*

Profound: If you had the chance to make a Native Tongue/Chicago supergroup who would be in it?

Dug Infinite: Still, living in Chicago? All Natural Crew, Bamski, Culture 45 Crew, Primeridian, Abstract Mindstate, Ang 13.

Profound: Word. Okay, lastly, how would you describe the Native Tongue influence on Hip-Hop and where do you rank them?

Dug Infinite: They have a 30-year-plus influence on the sound of Hip-Hop. They are still going too! I rank them in the top ten crews of all time.

Profound: I would like to personally thank you, Dug, for taking this time to answer our questions. You are always so gracious and giving to the culture. I am still a student of yours, and I continue to learn from you and appreciate all that you have done and continue to do.

Dug Infinite: Much Respect!!!!! Gratitude!!!!! Giving Thanks!!!!

FINAL WORDS

"Unfortunately, these kids, they'd rather listen to us kick it in a rhyme or a verse than listen to their own teacher at school. Being that they would rather listen to us we have to kick something else to them."

- Phife